DIVE SCAPA FLOW

DIVE
SCAPA FLOW

Rod Macdonald

MAINSTREAM
PUBLISHING

All rights reserved

MAINSTREAM PUBLISHING COMPANY (EDINBURGH) LTD
7 Albany Street
Edinburgh EH1 3UG

British Library Cataloguing in Publication Data

MacDonald, Rod
    Dive Scapa Flow
    1. Scotland. Orkney. Scapa Flow. Germany.
    Kriegsmarine. Warships, Underwater salvage
    I. Title
914.11′32

ISBN 1 85158 241 X

Typset by CR Barbers (Highlands) Ltd, Fort William, Scotland
Printed by Dotesios Ltd, Trowbridge

To Claire

CONTENTS

Acknowledgments   7

Preface   9

Introduction   11

1. Scapa Flow, 21 June 1919   15

2. Salvaging the High Seas Fleet   33

3. Diving the Scuttled German High Seas
    Fleet Today   53

4. The Individual Wrecks of the High Seas Fleet   67

5. Alternative Wreck Dives   98

6. Diving the Blockships   106

7. Scapa's War Graves – the Forbidden Wrecks   127

8. Travel, Accommodation and Dive-Boat
    Charters   143

Bibliography   156

Index   158

Acknowledgments

Covering as it does the many aspects of diving in Scapa Flow and the historical background of the many wrecks, it would have been impossible to have written this book without the help and encouragement that so many have freely given. It is only proper that I record here my heart-felt thanks to those people and in particular the following:

My wife, Claire, who bravely put up with me locking myself away in my study for long periods and for her enthusiasm and help with the research and her cut-away sketches of the German wrecks; Dick Cook, Ellon, who spent a considerable amount of his valuable time helping me to survey the wrecks and for the underwater photographs and many of the general photographs; Roderick and Agnes Mac-donald, Fraserburgh, who revised my early draft manuscripts; David Spence, Sandwick, Orkney, for the material and information he provided and the kindness and enthusiasm he displayed; Keith and Pearl Thomson, South Ronaldsay, for the help, hospitality and information they provided; Malcolm Foulis, Stronsay, who skippered the dive-boat on my last visit to Scapa Flow and freely gave so much practical information on the wrecks; Rob Ward, Illusion Illustration Ltd, Bridge of Muchalls, Stonehaven for the superb paintings of the sunken German warships; Ian Williamson, Aberdeen, for his meticulous graphics and cartography; Adam Gould, Dunfermline, and Mairi Caldwell, Aberdeen, for help in translating German documents; the staff at Stonehaven Public Library who bravely accommodated my continual requests for obscure and out-of-print reference books; the staff at The Orkney Library (OL), Kirkwall, for their kind help with reference books and for allowing me access to their photographic archive; The Imperial War Museum, London (IWM); Hydrographic Department, MoD, Taunton; Naval Historical Library, MoD, London.

Editor's Note
It has been difficult to decide as to whether we should use imperial or metric measurements in this book. We have compromised and have adopted the following plan:
  1. All ships' dimensions (length, beam and draught) are given in feet.
  2. All depths of, and distances across, the water are in metres, except where those run to miles.

ACKNOWLEDGMENTS

3. All historical details relating to armaments on the ships and so on are in inches or other appropriate imperial measures.

Preface

When I first dived the Scapa Flow wrecks I found that my first dive on any of the wrecks became something of a journey of exploration because nowhere was there any readily accessible source of information on them. There seemed to be no guide-book for divers that offered a history of the wrecks and, particularly, gave hard, practical and essential information on them. Every diver will be aware of the sense of anticipation mingled with apprehension that is felt as you drop down the shot-line on your first dive on a new wreck. You really don't know what to expect. The wreck could be lying on its side, its keel or even upside down. You don't know its condition or what will appear before your eyes out of the gloom. Each time I dived the Scapa Flow wrecks for the first time that is exactly how I felt. It was a case of confronting the unknown. That in a sense is exciting but in the underwater environment, when the distance you can see at any one time is often quite limited, it can be difficult to orientate yourself and recognise what it is you are diving on.

The purpose of this book is to fill that gap so that there is an easily readable book which both brings the wrecks alive by recounting the way in which these colossal German wrecks came to be at the bottom of Scapa Flow and at the same time is a factual guide to the present condition and displacement of the wrecks. I am greatly indebted to Rob Ward of Illusion Illustration Ltd for the superb paintings of the wrecks as they presently lie. These paintings were created from original photographs and diagrams of the vessels on the surface in all their glory and the information with which I was able to provide him after surveying the wrecks at some length with the aid of members of the Ellon Branch of the British Sub Aqua Club, of which I am a member.

For the first time ever, divers and non-divers alike are able to gaze upon these paintings and see exactly what the Scapa Flow wrecks are really like. A picture paints a thousand words and divers exploring the German wrecks will be able to see at a glance what they will be dropping on to. At the same time experienced divers will be able to recognise many familiar features from these paintings and pick out ones that they have not previously seen.

Chapters One and Two describe the momentous events that led to the scuttling of the German High Seas Fleet and the subsequent titanic task of the salvagers who raised most of them. Chapter Three is designed to give practical hints to divers who have not experienced diving at Scapa Flow before. There is really nothing with which to compare it around British coasts.

Chapter Four is a detailed guide to the scuttled German Fleet and offers a graphic and easily readable source of information for divers planning their next day's diving. Chapter Five covers wrecks other than the German Fleet that you are likely to dive during your stay in Orkney. Chapter Six is a guide to the many wartime 'blockships' that lie in the channels that lead into Scapa Flow. These fall into two real classes, the Burra Sound blockships and the Churchill Barrier blockships. The latter are in very shallow, murky water and are really only suitable as second dives, night dives and for those relatively rare days when bad weather prevents diving in the Flow itself. They make ideal, safe, training wreck dives for less experienced or novice divers. The Burra Sound blockships are a completely different story and if I overenthuse about them in the book please forgive me. They are deeper than the Churchill Barrier blockships and have average visibility of 20 to 30 metres. The fish life is abundant and friendly, often willing to be fed by hand. Feeding fish inside the skeleton of a wreck in 30-metre visibility is not what you expect to do at Scapa Flow but is one of the highlights of diving there. For photographers there is no better place in Scapa Flow.

Anyone who stays at Scapa Flow for any length of time cannot help but be moved by the appalling loss of life that has occurred here. It is only fitting in a book about the sea and Scapa Flow that their sacrifice be remembered, so I have recounted the stories of some of the most tragic losses in Chapter Seven.

Chapter Eight is a guide to getting there, where to stay when you are there and a listing of all the dive-boat charters working the Flow at the moment so as to make booking your holiday a simple task.

Good diving,
Rod Macdonald

Introduction

Scapa Flow is a dramatic and windswept expanse of water some 12 miles across, which is almost completely encircled by the islands of Orkney. On the land all around there are poignant reminders of Orkney's war-torn past. Deserted barracks and gun emplacements bear silent witness to its military history. For centuries Scapa Flow has been a safe, sheltered and heavily defended anchorage for the Royal Navy. Great warships and dramatic deeds are an integral part of that past. In the First and Second World Wars the main Atlantic Operations HQ was set up at the naval base of Lyness. It is, however, what lies beneath the waves of Scapa Flow that is making Orkney a magnet for today's sports divers.

In a single, momentous event on 21 June 1919, the entire German Imperial Navy's High Seas Fleet was scuttled to avoid it falling into the hands of the British. It was the single greatest piece of naval suicide the world has ever seen. Seventy-four great warships slowly sank to the bottom of Scapa Flow to litter the sea-bed. Initially the Admiralty resolved to leave the sunken fleet to rust on the bottom of the Flow forever. After the end of the First World War there was so much scrap metal about that it was not economically viable to salvage them. By the 1920s the price of scrap had picked up and the salvagers' attention was turned to the seemingly endless supply of best German scrap metal at the bottom of Scapa Flow. Over the course of the coming decades the majority of the warships were salvaged and today only eight of the original fleet remain on the sea-bed waiting to be explored. They are the 26,000-ton battleships *König*, *Markgraf* and *Kronprinz Wilhelm*, the 5,000-ton light cruisers *Dresden*, *Brummer*, *Köln* and *Karlsruhe* and the 900-ton destroyer *V 83*.

Over the years many other vessels have come to grief in Scapa Flow. Steamers and tugs have struck mines. Attacking U-boats have been depth-charged and trawlers have succumbed to the fierce northern gales. The scale of human loss in Scapa Flow is huge.

The 19,560-ton British battleship *Vanguard* was destroyed in one cataclysmic magazine explosion on 9 July 1917 with the loss of more than 700 men.

A U-boat managed to slip past the British defences on 14 October 1939 in the dead of night and torpedo the 29,000-ton

British battleship *Royal Oak* at anchor. The *Royal Oak* turned turtle within five minutes and sank in 30 metres of water with most of her crew trapped inside her. The torpedo explosions destroyed the power circuits and the whole of the ship below decks was pitched into darkness. Desperately the crew stumbled around in the darkness groping for a way out as the ship keeled over. Flash fires of burning cordite swept round the corridors. In all, 833 officers and men died in that one attack. (These two latter wrecks are war graves and no diving is permitted on them.)

During the First and Second World Wars, 'blockships' were sunk in some of the channels leading into the Flow to place immovable and insurmountable barriers in the way of any enemy vessel trying to get into the Flow to attack British shipping.

Today this concentrated profusion of wrecks in one relatively small area has led to a boom in diving at Scapa Flow. Thousand of divers visit the Flow annually, coming from all over the UK, Europe and the United States. Diving has become big business in Orkney and there are more than ten full-time dive-boats operating in the Flow from April through to October.

The diving at Scapa Flow is deep and exhilarating. The German High Seas Fleet is in 30 to 45 metres of water and for novices and experienced divers alike the heart races as you jump from the safety and warmth of the dive-boat into the water. Once in the water the visibility averages about 12 metres so the weighted shot-line seems to disappear straight below into infinity in a bottomless pit. The wrecks are far below out of sight. As divers descend, pressure on their ears is felt, much the same as in planes only more pronounced. Divers must ensure that they clear their ears and equalise the pressure by 'popping' them. A failure to do this would soon lead to a burst eardrum. Once a diver passes deeper than about ten metres the increase in water pressure becomes more intense, squeezing the diver's suit against his body. The suit loses some of its buoyancy and the diver effectively becomes heavier. The equilibrium is restored by the diver bleeding air from his air cylinder into his suit or alternatively into his life-jacket which doubles as a buoyancy compensator.

The descent down to the wrecks seems to take forever and as the distance from the surface increases so the natural light fades. Slowly the gloom below seems to acquire a form. The huge shape of the wreck seems to materialise out of the darkness. The German wrecks either lie on their sides or upside-down, so it is usually a flat piece of hull that comes into view first. After a check on your gauges to ensure everything is in order, you can swim to the side of the hull and look down the now vertical deck. Because of their size, the wrecks cast a considerable shadow and on the dark side it appears at first completely black. Dropping over the side and free-falling down the vertical deck your eyes become accustomed to the darkness and soon you hardly notice any difference as you drift spellbound over the virtually intact wrecks. Everywhere you look there is something of interest. Gun-turrets loom up in front of you. Anchor chains are still run out from their chain lockers to the steam-driven deck capstans before dropping vertically down to the sea-bed. The armoured bridges are always a source of fascination for divers. Immediately behind the bridge are empty lifeboat davits. The lifeboats themselves were lowered over the side by the German sailors as the vessels scuttled and they made good their escape. Rows of portholes line the hulls and the wrecks are festooned with a rich carpet of marine growth. Innumerable open hatchways and companionways entice divers inside. To do so is potentially fatal. Only properly experienced divers, fully equipped with ropes and lights, should even consider penetrating the cavernous interiors of these wrecks. Fine silt layers the corridors inside and careless finning easily stirs it up. Divers can become engulfed in a cloud of silt and the visibility can be reduced to nil. In this situation it may be impossible to find your way out and panic will quickly set in.

At this depth a diver's air supply is quickly used up and all too soon it is time to ascend. As you float slowly upwards the now familiar lines of the warship blur and then once again merge with the background as you leave this silent, eerie world far below and return to the surface and daylight.

Diving is a fast-growing sport and correspondingly the number of divers visiting Orkney each year is increasing. Once you have dived Scapa Flow you will always hanker to come back. Scapa Flow's attraction is fascinating. The wrecks are so big, on average 500 to 600 feet long, that on one dive you will only be able to explore a small part of them. It would take a dozen dives really to get to know any one wreck here. This, coupled with the unequalled profusion of wrecks, means that you will always leave Scapa Flow with many of the wrecks undived. The diving is deep. It is exhilarating, and if done sensibly will give some of the best wreck-diving around.

Scapa Flow, 21 June 1919

Dawn had come early. The slow, creeping arrival of daylight filtering over the horizon had heralded the start of a beautiful day at the deep naval anchorage of Scapa Flow. Shielded on all sides from the fury of the Atlantic by its islands, the sea in this natural harbour some ten miles across was calm and exceptionally blue. The sky above was clear. There in the Flow the coming of daylight unveiled a majestic and formidable sight but one which residents had become used to over the preceding seven months. They hardly gave a second thought to the sight that greeted anyone looking out over the water. For there in the Flow at anchor lay the 74 grey warships of the interned German Imperial Navy's High Seas Fleet. They lay motionless, moored in neat rows, dominating the skyline with their very size and dwarfing the smaller tender vessels that chugged around them. They had lain there, immobile, for the previous seven months.

The interned Fleet was made up of five battlecruisers, 11 battleships, eight cruisers and 50 destroyers. Built up over the preceding 20 years in a naval arms race with Britain, the High Seas Fleet had been created at huge cost to the German nation to challenge the traditional naval supremacy of Britain. The assembled might of the High Seas Fleet, however, no longer represented a potent fighting force. The great warships were manned only by skeleton crews. Their guns had been disarmed and they were covered in surface rust and marine growths from their long stay at anchor in the Flow. The Fleet ranged from the massive 656-foot long 26,000-ton battlecruisers *Seydlitz, Moltke, Von Der Tann, Derfflinger* and *Hindenburg*, to the smaller 24,000-ton battleships such as the *Kronprinz Wilhelm* and *König*, to the light cruisers of about 5,000 tons such as the *Köln* and *Dresden* and finally to the torpedo-boat destroyers.

In amongst these mighty vessels a few British patrol boats and tenders moved around. Elements of the British Grand Fleet were normally moored in the Flow to guard the German Fleet but that morning the hand of fate had dealt an ace to Rear-Admiral Ludwig von Reuter who was in charge of the German High Seas Fleet. The British Grand Fleet would leave Scapa

Flow for the first time in the seven long months of internment to carry out an exercise at sea.

High Seas Fleet at anchor, taken from Houghton Bay

The mighty force of the German Fleet had not surrendered to the British. It had not been crushed in a sea battle with Britain. It had been 'interned' at Scapa Flow for those seven long, dismal months as a condition of the Armistice which had suspended hostilities in the closing months of the First World War. The German land forces had been defeated. Their leaders were pressing for surrender terms with the Allies and the High Seas Fleet was proving to be a pawn in those negotiations. Constructed at enormous cost and maintained at a similarly high cost throughout the war, it had been a big drain on Germany's resources and yet had neither really proved itself in battle nor suffered heavy losses. There had been only one major sea battle between the opposing British and German fleets, the Battle of Jutland, which, although costly in terms of casualties and damage inflicted, resolved nothing. The German Fleet had survived the war relatively intact and could still have posed a very real threat to the Allies if the peace negotiations were to break down and

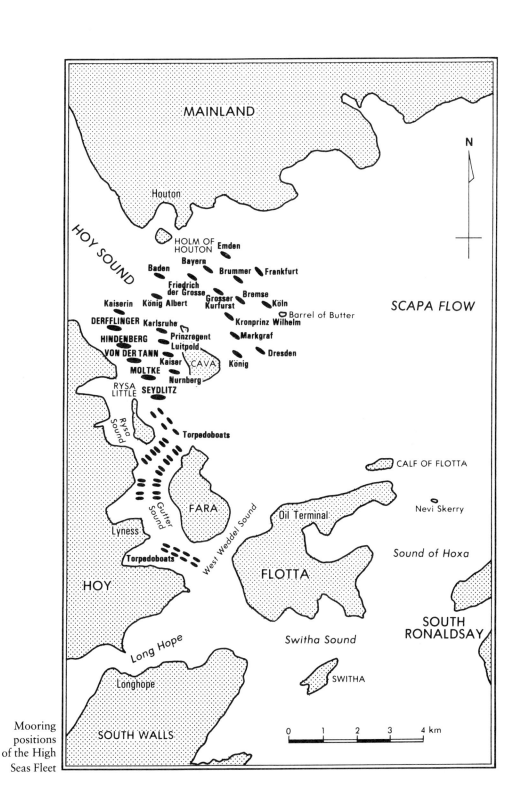

MAINLAND

Houton

HOY SOUND

HOLM OF HOUTON

Emden
Bayern
Baden   Brummer   Frankfurt
Friedrich   Bremse
der Grosse   Grosser
Kaiserin   König Albert   Kurfurst   Köln
DERFFLINGER   Karlsruhe   Barrel of Butter
HINDENBERG   Prinzregent   Kronprinz Wilhelm
VON DER TANN   Luitpold   Markgraf
                  Kaiser   CAVA   König   Dresden
MOLTKE   Nurnberg
RYSA
LITTLE   SEYDLITZ

Ryso
Sound   Torpedoboats

SCAPA FLOW

CALF OF FLOTTA

Gutter
Sound   FARA   Oil Terminal   Nevi Skerry

Lyness   West Weddel Sound   Sound of Hoxa

Torpedoboats   FLOTTA

HOY   SOUTH
                                   RONALDSAY

Long Hope   Switha Sound

Longhope   SWITHA

Mooring
positions
of the High   SOUTH WALLS   0   1   2   3   4 km
Seas Fleet

N

hostilities recommence.

The Fleet had effectively become a bargaining counter in the peace negotiations and whilst those negotiations dragged on, the Fleet was, as a condition of the Armistice, to be kept interned under the close guard of the Allies. In effect, the High Seas Fleet was being held hostage. Eventually the peace negotiations would form the basis of the Treaty of Versailles which formally ended the First World War.

Once the Armistice had been called, arrangements were made by the Allies to receive the German High Seas Fleet into internment. The entire British Grand Fleet had met the German High Seas Fleet in the North Sea to escort it into Scapa Flow. No such sea force had ever been gathered before — 90,000 men on 370 warships. The British were taking no chances on any German treachery. Their guns were loaded and the crews were at action stations alertly looking out for any signs of trouble. The British Grand Fleet formed a passage of two lines of battleships, six miles apart and stretching beyond sight into the distance. The German High Seas Fleet had sailed through this passage in single column and been escorted by the British Grand Fleet into internment.

The warships, although under Allied guard, remained German property. By June 1919, they were manned only by skeleton German crews of up to 200 on the larger vessels. The bulk of the 20,000 German sailors who had brought the ships to British waters had been repatriated. There were no British guards on board and the ships were prohibited from flying the German Imperial Navy ensign with its black cross and eagle.

9 a.m. The British battleships of the Grand Fleet sailed out of the Flow with their supporting cruisers and destroyers, leaving only two serviceable destroyers on guard duty.

10 a.m. Rear-Admiral Ludwig von Reuter, in command of the German High Seas Fleet, appeared in full dress uniform on the quarter-deck of his flagship, the cruiser *Emden*. He proudly bore the insignia of his highest decorations around his neck. The Iron Cross and his other medals were pinned to the breast of his frock-coat. One of his attendant officers approached, saluted and spoke with him for a short period. After that conversation had ended the Admiral paced up and down the quarter-deck, often stopping to study the other ships in the formation through his telescope. One of his staff advised him that the British battleships on guard duty had left the Flow with their supporting cruisers and destroyers on an

SMS *Emden*, *Frankfurt* and *Bremse* enter Scapa Flow, 25 November 1918 (IWM)

exercise earlier that morning. He could hardly believe his luck.

Reuter issued an order that the international code flags 'DG' be raised on the *Emden*, his flagship. This signal alerted the officers of the other ships of the Fleet that they were to man their bridges and keep a special look-out for further signals. Reuter was aware from copies of four-day-old newspapers given to him by the British that the Armistice was to have ended this day and suspected that the British would try to seize the Fleet if the peace negotiations did not bring about a satisfactory final agreement before the Armistice ended. The papers he had read indicated that no agreement was likely and he knew that the breakdown of the peace negotiations could only result in hostilities being recommenced. Unbeknown to him, however, the Armistice had been extended by two days, to 7 p.m. on Monday, 23 June. The British Grand Fleet was under orders to be back in the Flow by then to deal with any trouble that might arise should the Armistice not be further extended.

10.30 a.m. Rear Admiral von Reuter addressed an attendant signaller and shortly afterwards a string of command flags appeared over his ship even although this was well outwith the permitted times for issuing signals. The order read:

'*PARAGRAPH II.* BESTÄTIGEN.' ('Paragraph eleven. Confirm.')

SMS *Bayern* down
by the stern (IWM)

The Admiral continued studying his ships. The prearranged coded order to the commanders of the other ships in the Fleet to scuttle their vessels had just been given. The details of the plan to scuttle the Fleet had been finalised four days earlier on 17 June. The Germans knew that if the British did try to seize the Fleet little opposition could be offered. With only skeleton crews remaining aboard and the guns disarmed, the Fleet was not an effective fighting force in its present condition. Unbeknown to Reuter the Allies had formulated just such a seizure plan months before as part of their contingency planning.

The signal to scuttle was repeated from ship to ship by semaphore and by Morse code on signal lamps. In this fashion it travelled slowly around the Fleet. The southernmost ships of the long lines of destroyers were not visible from the flagship, *Emden*. They had to wait for a full hour until the order reached them. The prearranged formal responses came back, slowly to begin with. The first reached the *Emden* at about 11.30 a.m., just as the original signal reached the last of the destroyers: 'Paragraph eleven is confirmed.'

Reuter's own ship, the *Emden*, was one of the last to start scuttling. He had delayed giving the order to scuttle his own vessel because two British drifters and a water supply vessel were alongside his flagship collecting stores and replenishing his own vessel with water. Reuter was in a dilemma. He could not give the order to scuttle with the British vessels alongside. They would have been able to take immediate action to stop the *Emden* going to the bottom by boarding and closing its flood valves. They might even have rumbled the whole plan and been able to summon help and thwart the entire operation. He had to sweat it out until they left even although the rest of the Fleet was now beginning to put the order into effect. His own crew went about their work completely unaware of the drama unfolding around them because for security reasons none other than trusted officers had been told of the plan to scuttle. Eventually Reuter would be able to give the order to scuttle the vessel to Lieutenant-Commander Ehlers at 12.10 p.m.

In a patriotic gesture of defiance many of the German ships ran up the Imperial Navy ensign at their sterns. The prohibited white flags with their bold black cross and eagle had not been seen at Scapa Flow before. Others ran up the red flag, the letter 'Z', which in international code signalled: 'Advance on the enemy.'

Noon An artist, who had hitched a ride on one of the patrolling British Navy trawlers to sketch the assembled might of the German Fleet at anchor, noticed that small boats were being lowered down the side of some of the German ships, against British standing orders, and told a British officer. Sixteen minutes later the first of the warships to sink, the *Friedrich der Grosse*, turned turtle and went to the bottom. The other ships in the Fleet began to list as the water rushing into their innards altered their buoyancy. For the last four days, Reuter's trusted sailors had been opening all the doors and hatches and fixing them in that position to enable them to flood more easily. The sea-cocks were set on a hair turning and lubricated very thoroughly. Large hammers had been placed beside any valves that would allow water to flood in if knocked off. The sea-valves were now opened and disconnected from the upper deck to prevent the British closing them if they boarded a ship before it went down. Sea-water pipes were smashed and condensers opened. Bulkhead rivets were prised out. Once the valves and sea-cocks were open their keys and handles were thrown overboard. They could never be closed again and so, once the vessels had started to scuttle, they could not be stopped other than by being taken in tow and beached.

Some of the great vessels rolled slowly on to their sides

while others went down by the bow or stern first, forcing the other end of the vessel to lift high out of the water. Others sank on an even keel. Some had been moored in shallower water and settled quickly into the cold waters to rest on the sea-bed leaving only their masts and funnels standing proud of the water. Blasts of steam, oil and air roared out of the ships' vents and white clouds of vapour billowed up from the sides of the ships. Great anchor chains, which had been run out to hold the ships in position, snapped with the strain and crashed into the sea or whiplashed against the decks and sides of the ships. The ships groaned and protested as they were subjected to stresses and strains for which they had never been designed. Their immense steel hulls reared up at the stern or bow and slanted over to slide beneath the surface.

As each vessel passed from sight a whirlpool was created. Debris swirled around in it, slowly being sucked inwards and eventually, relentlessly, being pulled under into the murky depths. Gradually, oil escaping from the submerged ships spread upwards and outwards to cover the surface of the sea with a dark film. Scattered across the Flow were boats, hammocks, lifebelts, chests, spars, matchwood and debris. A human drama unfolded as hundreds of German sailors abandoned ship and struggled for their lives in the cold waters of the Flow. Other German sailors lined upon the deck of one of the largest ships to cheer a farewell to another ship close by as it slid beneath the waves. One German sailor was even seen to dance a hornpipe on the deck of the *Baden*.

The British force guarding the interned fleet, the First Battle Squadron commanded by Sir Sydney Fremantle, consisted of five battleships, two light cruisers and nine destroyers. For the first time in the seven months of internment, they had left the Flow earlier that morning to carry out a long-range torpedo-firing exercise at sea. A small guard force of three British destroyers, the *Vegar*, the *Vesper* and an unserviceable destroyer, the *Victorious*, had been left behind. When Fremantle learned of the attempted scuttle he immediately ordered his ships to return to the Flow at full speed. The first would only be able to get back at around 2 p.m. The last would arrive back at about 4 p.m., by which time only three German battleships, three light cruisers and a few destroyers would still be afloat out of the total interned force of 74 warships.

When it was initially ascertained that the entire High Seas Fleet had started to scuttle, panic and mayhem broke out amongst the crews of the British guard vessels in the Flow. They quickly realised the enormity of what was being done

The destroyer *S 137* scuttled at Scapa Flow (IWM)

and how impotent they were to stop it. The two British destroyers, the *Vegar* and the *Vesper*, steamed into the channel between Hoy and Fara, reaching the tail-end of the ranks of torpedo boats. They opened fire as they closed and shots rang out from small arms, machine-guns and larger guns. Three Germans, in a lifeboat containing 13 men, were killed and four were wounded. The others were ordered back on board and forced by threats of further shooting to turn off the flood valves. A stoker in the lifeboat of the *V 127* was shot in the stomach and died shortly afterwards. A British drifter was seen towing two or three lifeboats full of German sailors. One of them stood up and tried to cut his boat free from the tow rope. A Royal Marine raised his rifle and shot him dead. The British in all managed to beach three ships of the torpedo-boat flotilla. Five others sank in shallow water and remained visible, with their superstructure standing proud of the water.

A British drifter put an armed boarding party aboard the battleship *Markgraf*. The captain, Lt-Cdr Walther Schumann, was assisting with the final procedures necessary to ensure the sinking of his vessel. He delayed as long as he could and then emerged to meet the boarding party waving a white flag. He refused to obey an order from the boarding party to order his own men to go below and shut off the flood valves or to allow the boarders to do so. The boarding party had its orders and a scuffle broke out in which Schumann was shot through the head and died immediately. Another officer was seriously wounded. Others of his crew, however,

stayed below to complete the work. Enough had been done to send the *Markgraf* to the bottom where she lies today.

In all, nine German sailors would die that day. Their graves can still be seen at the naval cemetery at Lyness on Hoy. Sixteen others were wounded. These killings seem inspired by feelings among the British sailors of panic, anger and impotence at their inability to prevent most of the vessels sinking. The Flow echoed to the sound of gunfire. Several lifeboats were fired on in the confusion. Shots came from the land as soldiers, marines and locals repelled lifeboats filled with German sailors seeking to land on the shore. On the island of Cava a group of women wielding pitchforks and other farm tools managed to scare off a party of Germans who were trying to land on the beach.

The *Emden* still had the British drifters, which had been helping to replenish her stores, alongside her. Once the *Friedrich der Grosse* went to the bottom and the other ships in the Fleet had started to settle down into the water, the crews of the drifters still alongside the *Emden* made to cast off. The Germans aboard her, however, held their mooring ropes long enough to enable their comrades to throw their hastily assembled kitbags on to the drifters and abandon the *Emden* by shinning down the mooring ropes into them.

British tug alongside the scuttled destroyer *G 102*. A British rating is pulling down the German flags and ensign (IWM)

Reuter decided to go ashore to find the senior British officer to try to get the shooting stopped. The officer whom he really wanted to get hold of had in fact left Lyness aboard the *Victorious* for the scene of the scuttling and Reuter was met only by a young British officer who did not have the necessary authority to get it stopped. Reuter therefore went back aboard the drifter and headed back towards the *Emden*. In all the confusion, the drifter ran aground on a shoal in a bay on the coast of Cava. By about 1.30 p.m. she had managed to get off and steam back into the Flow. As she did so her crew saw the battlecruiser *Grosser Kurfürst* succumbing to the weight of the in-rushing water and slipping under the surface into the black depths. As she went she raised steeply into the air and then crashed downwards on to her port side. Her two towering masts hit the water only a matter of yards away from an onlooking British vessel. The blackened mouths of the funnels looked like caverns into which tons of green sea-water flooded. She then turned and went under.

2 p.m. Fremantle's main group, returning from their aborted exercise, steamed hurriedly into the Flow, surging through the water. They charged in at 22 knots smashing through the short seas of the Flow, a spectacle of power and aggression. One destroyer broke off from the main group and cut the sinking *Emden*'s anchor cable. She attempted to tow her towards the shore and safety. By beaching her she could be saved and in time refloated. If she went down in the deeper waters of the Flow where she had been anchored then there would be little hope of salvaging her in the short term. The attempt was successful. Some of Fremantle's destroyers fired salvoes of shells from their big guns. Presumably these were meant as warning shots because nothing was hit. Armed boarding parties went aboard the *Baden* to try and stop the flood of water into her. They managed to restart the diesel generation units, giving light and enabling systematic pumping to start.

The leader of the destroyer group, Captain McLean, threatened any German commander whose ship sank with summary execution. A number of German officers were lined up by the British on the torpedo-boat destroyer *S 132* of the Sixth Torpedo-boat Flotilla. A Royal Marine firing squad was drawn up but no executions in fact took place. A man described in contemporary accounts as 'an English civilian', but probably an off-duty officer who had hastily returned to his ship from ashore, boarded another German destroyer and put a pistol to the head of a German officer. He pulled the trigger . . . and missed. In the heat of the moment the barrel had slipped and the officer survived with a bad cut, muzzle-blast burns and a loud ringing in his ears.

Reuter went next to the *Bayern*, picking up men from lifeboats on the way. The *Bayern* was eventually to keel over, turn turtle and plunge to the bottom of the Flow at about 2.30 p.m. Another British destroyer took the *Bremse* in tow in an effort to beach her. She capsized and sank as Reuter looked on and the British destroyer had to cut its towing cable to avoid being endangered herself.

Apart from the *Emden*, two light cruisers did not sink. The *Frankfurt* was beached only in the nick of time as the waters of the Flow began to wash her decks. The *Nürnberg* was also run aground after another British destroyer had severed her anchor chain with high explosives and towed her to safety ashore. The five remaining light cruisers, the *Karlsruhe, Köln, Dresden, Brummer* and *Bremse*, all went to the bottom and, all except the *Bremse*, remain for today's divers to explore. The drifter *Clonsin* had taken the *Dresden* in tow even although she was so low in the water that her main deck was awash. Painfully slowly the *Clonsin* made for the beach on the island of Cava less than a mile away. On the way the *Dresden* lurched down by the head and then capsized and sank so quickly that there was no time to cast off the towing cable.

On the 24,600-ton battle-cruiser *Seydlitz*, the entire crew stood proudly to attention on the deck singing the German national anthem and watching as the *Moltke* sank beside them. They then had to abandon their own ship and 40 minutes later the *Seydlitz* followed the *Moltke* to the bottom. Reuter had by this time given up the idea of going aboard a German ship and with his personal staff went aboard the British destroyer *Revenge* at about 4 p.m.

As the once proud ships of the German High Seas Fleet either sank or were saved by beaching, some order seemed to emerge from the chaos. Scapa Flow, which only hours before had seen one of the greatest assemblages of naval firepower in history, now only bore the scars of this unparalleled act of self-destruction. Calm returned to the scene. As far as the eye could see the surface was littered with floating debris. Slicks of oil spread inexorably outwards. Small ships' boats full of German sailors were rowed through the flotsam and in each a man held a single white flag. Empty lifeboats rocked in the calm sea. The sea-bed was littered with sunken battleships and every now and then a bubble of trapped air would escape

The SMS *Bayern* slips slowly beneath the waves (IWM)

German prisoners aboard the quarter-deck of HMS *Ramillies* (IWM)

from one of the submerged giants and rise upwards to break the surface. British patrol boats moved slowly around, sometimes taking wallowing lifeboats in tow.

That evening the homeless German sailors were split up amongst the five British battleships. The British Commanding Officer, Fremantle, issued an order that the Germans should be treated with 'minimum courtesy'. This order was strictly obeyed by the British. German kitbags were allegedly searched and pillaged, with watches and knives being stolen. Some German sailors were beaten up. On the *Resolution* the ninth German sailor was shot and later died. Even Reuter's Admiral's cloak was stolen by a British sailor.

Aboard the *Revenge*, a short and bitter exchange took place between Fremantle and Reuter. Reuter tried to explain that he had given the order to scuttle as he genuinely believed that the Armistice was to have ended that day and that hostilities were about to recommence between Germany and the Allies. He had taken this information from a four-day-old newspaper that had been issued as normal to the Germans by the British. It was thought that the Germans could not learn anything that they might use to their advantage from these old newspapers, but they were avidly read as they were one of the few means the Germans had of keeping up with what was going on in the outside world. The German sailors were not allowed off their vessels and could glean no information from local sources. All their wireless receivers had some time earlier been collected and taken away by the British. Their only other real source of information was from conversations with the crews of supply vessels that came from Germany regularly to replenish the Fleet. The Allies had insisted, at the very beginning of the Armistice talks, that the Germans would have to be responsible for supplying the Fleet whilst it was in internment. They were provided with water, coal and oil by the British as they recognised the insurmountable difficulties that supplying these essentials to the 74 ships of the Fleet from Germany would entail. Reuter claimed to be amazed when he was advised that the Armistice had in fact been extended by two days. Fremantle always maintained that he had informed Reuter 'unofficially' of the extension before the scuttling, but Reuter continually denied having any knowledge of it prior to the evening of 21 June 1919. The argument got nowhere and broke up.

That night, the British battleships, laden with the 1,774 homeless German officers and men, set off southwards from the Flow bound for Nigg in the Cromarty Firth. They had

German sailors supplement their rations by fishing from the deck of an interned destroyer (IWM)

been classified as prisoners-of-war by Fremantle and were given little comfort on the voyage. They had to sleep that night where they could find a space. Most slept on the cold steel decks despite being wet through from the day's enforced dip in the cold waters of the Flow. Others slept in gun turrets. Some managed to sleep below decks out of the cold sea air.

At Nigg they were to be handed over officially from naval custody into military custody. Ironically, the procedure for the handover had been worked out some months before as part of Fremantle's contingency plans for seizing the entire German Fleet if the peace negotiations broke down and hostilities recommenced.

The squadron arrived at noon the following day and dropped anchor. Reuter and his staff were escorted back to the deck of the *Revenge* and led into a square of armed Royal Marines and other British ratings. The German and British officers stood face to face, staring coldly at each other. Fremantle appeared and read a prepared speech from a piece of paper in his hand. The speeches are recounted in Dan van der Vat's book *The Grand Scuttle*.

> Admiral von Reuter, I cannot permit you and your officers to leave naval custody without expressing to you my sense of the manner in which you have violated common honour and the honourable traditions of seamen of all nations. With an Armistice

in full operation you recommenced hostilities without notice by hoisting the German flag in the interned ships and proceeding to sink and destroy them. You have informed my interpreter that you considered the Armistice had terminated. You had no justification whatever for that assumption. You would have been informed by me of the termination of the Armistice and whether the representatives of your nation had or had not signed the Treaty of Peace. Indeed, letters in readiness to send to you to that effect as soon as I had received official intimation from my Government were written and signed. Further, can you possibly suppose that my squadron would have been out of harbour at the moment of the termination of the Armistice? By your conduct you have added one more to the breaches of faith and honour of which Germany has been guilty in this war. Begun with a breach of military honour in the invasion of Belgium it bids fair to terminate with a breach of naval honour. You have proved to the few who doubted it that the word of the new Germany is no more to be trusted than that of the old. What opinion your country will form of your action I do not know. I can only express what I believe to be the opinion of the British Navy, and indeed of all seamen except those of your nation. I now transfer you to the custody of the British military authorities as prisoners-of-war, guilty of a flagrant violation of the Armistice.

The German officers remained standing stiffly to attention as an interpreter translated the address to Reuter. Reuter made a curt reply in German.

Tell your Admiral that I am unable to agree with the burden of his speech and that our understanding of the matter differs. I alone carry the responsibility. I am convinced that any English naval officer placed as I was would have acted in the same way.

The Germans then clicked their heels, turned and went back down the accommodation ladder.

The Germans prisoners spent the night ashore at Nigg and were then moved southwards by train to prisoner-of-war camps in the north of England. Most German accounts agree that the Seaforth Highlanders behaved generally in a proper manner. Some of them, however, patently did not. There were reports of German prisoners' possessions being looted at bayonet point. Some ugly incidents took place at railway stations on the way as hostile crowds of off-duty soldiers, women and children spat and jeered at the prisoners. Punches were aimed at them and stones were thrown. Reuter himself was taken under a British military escort to a bank to change money. A boisterous crowd of about 1,000 people quickly formed round about him shouting abuse. Reuter was struck on the shoulder by a woman, and a lump of coal thrown from the crowd hit him in the face.

Whilst the British reaction was hostile, the German Press acclaimed the scuttling as the last heroic act of the German Navy. Reuter managed to get his explanation for the scuttling out of his prisoner-of-war camp to his superiors in Germany by having an officer, who was due to be repatriated, memorise it for subsequent repetition to the German Admiralty on his return. The officer's repatriation was unfortunately delayed and he was only able to pass on the message in mid-August. The account disclosed to his superiors that one of Reuter's main reasons for ordering the scuttle was a standing order that on no account were German ships to be allowed to fall into enemy hands in time of war. This meant that if Germany had rejected the peace terms being offered by the Allies and an attempt was made to seize the ships, they would have to be sunk. This was the only form of effective opposition to the British left open to Reuter. If, on the other hand, Germany had signed the peace treaty the Fleet would have been surrendered.

Reuter explained that he had only become aware on 20 June of the official text of the German counter-proposals to the Allied peace terms from an old copy of *The Times* newspaper of 16 June passed to him by the British. From this he had seen that the German Fleet was to be used as a bargaining factor in the peace negotiations. That night he tried to get a wireless message transmitted to the German Government asking for an order that the officers be relieved of their duties before the surrender. The message was passed to Fremantle only on the morning of 21 June and was never sent. After that, Reuter saw a copy of *The Times* of 17 June containing the official Allied response to Germany which included a refusal to accept any of the German counter-proposals. The Germans had been given five days to accept. Reuter had to conclude therefore that if the Peace Treaty was not signed by Saturday 21 June then a state of war would once more exist between the Allies and the German nation. Judging from the tone of the speeches reported in *The Times* it appeared to him that there was no possibility of an agreement. He had allegedly been given no information about the extension of the Armistice period although Fremantle always maintained that he had told him. For these reasons Reuter gave the order to scuttle the interned Fleet on Saturday 21 June.

The Admiralty subsequently attempted on two occasions to bring Reuter to trial. On both occasions the proposed trial was ruled to be incompetent. The High Seas Fleet, although interned, had not been surrendered and consequently remained German property. A German Admiral could hardly be tried by the British for destroying German property over which the British had no legal right. The British had no jurisdiction over the Fleet. To the British the fact that Reuter was beyond legal reprisals made the scuttling even more frustrating and the British Press freely and fiercely pilloried him.

In the autumn of 1919 the Allies presented their demands for reparations for the scuttled ships in detail, by way of a Protocol to the Treaty of Versailles which had officially ended the war. Five light cruisers were to be surrendered within 60 days and 400,000 tons of dock equipment within 90 days. The *B 98*, a German re-supply vessel which had arrived at Scapa Flow after the Fleet had been scuttled, was to be retained and the crews of the scuttled ships were to be repatriated on fulfilment of the first two demands at the latest. They effectively became hostages to ensure that Germany complied with the reparation demands. After a lot of indecisive squabbling, Germany eventually signed the Protocol on reparations on 10 January 1920.

Reuter and a few others had been held in a prisoner-of-war camp since the scuttling seven months earlier. Once the Protocol had been signed he and the others were taken by train to Hull where the German steamer *Lisboa* took them homewards across the North Sea towards Wilhelmshaven. They were the last German prisoners-of-war to be repatriated. A flotilla of German destroyers greeted the steamer *en route* and escorted it back to an emotional welcome home at the port where a band played rousing military music and cheering groups of soldiers, sailors, veterans and civilians waited.

The German sailors who had been shot that fateful day, 21 June 1919, were the last casualties of the First World War. The Great War officially ended on 28 June 1919, only seven days after the might of the German Fleet had sunk dramatically to the bottom of Scapa Flow.

* A graphic and concise account of the naval arms race that led to the formation of the German and British Fleets, the run up to internment, the scuttling and its aftermath can be found in *The Grand Scuttle* by Dan van der Vat.

Salvaging the
High Seas Fleet

In the *mêlée* that had followed Reuter's order to scuttle, the Royal Navy successfully managed to beach the battleship *Baden*, the light cruisers *Emden*, *Frankfurt* and *Nürnberg*, and 18 destroyers. The other 52 warships which made up the High Seas Fleet were successfully scuttled by the Germans. Of those 52 ships that did go to the bottom, 45 were successfully raised from their watery graves by the greatest marine salvage operation in history. The salvaging started in the 1920s and continued until 1946. Today, eight warships of that Fleet remain on the bottom of Scapa Flow for divers to explore.

The British Admiralty's initial reaction to the scuttling was that the ships would be left to rot on the bottom of Scapa Flow where they had come to rest. There was to be no question of salvaging them. Naval salvage experts concluded unwisely that the wrecks would not prove to be any danger to shipping. They were soon proved wrong as almost immediately local vessels started snagging and going aground on their submerged hulls. In fact, on the very day of the scuttling itself, a British drifter, *Ramna*, went aground on the hull of the battle-cruiser *Moltke*, which was only just covered at high water. When the tide turned she was left high and dry on the battle-cruiser's now exposed hull.

The huge war effort had created a vast abundance of scrap metal in the form of armaments, shell-casings and the like, which now had no useful purpose, so economically there was no profit to be made in raising the huge German vessels from their resting places in the depths. By 1922, however, the market for scrap metal had started to pick up and one of the destroyers lying in shallower water was brought to the surface and taken to Stromness for breaking up. After this the Admiralty changed its mind and invited tenders for salvaging some of the ships. The Admiralty sold off the scuttled destroyers cheaply, at a price of £250 each. The battleships were later sold off for £1,000.

The first salvage attempts were basic as no one had any experience of a salvage undertaking of this magnitude. One of the first attempts was made by a Mr J. W. Robertson whose company, the Scapa Flow Salvage and Shipping Company Ltd,

HM drifter *Ramna* stranded on the submerged hull of the battlecruiser *Moltke* (IWM)

purchased two concrete barges from the Admiralty and set up a framework of steel girders across the gap between them. Two huge buoyancy bags were attached to the sunken vessel, one at each side. Steel cables were then threaded under the ship and chains attached to either end. These chains could be wound in and, together with the lift generated by the lifting bags, it was hoped that this would manage to pull the ship free from the clinging mud. The theory was that once free from the suction of the muddy sea-bed, the warship could then float to the surface. The theory was to prove successful in practice on the smaller ships.

The next attempts were made by Mr Ernest Cox and his company, Cox and Danks Ltd. His name was to become synonymous with the salvage works at Scapa Flow. Already a wealthy man before he started, Cox would spend eight painstaking and frustrating years working at Scapa Flow. His efforts gained world-wide interest and he succeeded in his dream of raising a large part of the sunken Fleet. He became obsessed with lifting the colossal *Hindenburg*. After many failed attempts he was to realise his ambition. She was the largest vessel ever salvaged. For all this time and effort he ended up £10,000 down over the eight-year period!

Cox initially bought the *Seydlitz* and *Hindenburg* from the Admiralty and then went on to buy the rest of the Fleet to earn him the title of 'the Man who bought a Navy'. When Cox made his decision to lift the Fleet he had never salvaged anything in his life before. He was just an enterprising scrap metal merchant. He had no knowledge of practical salvage techniques and he wasn't even a qualified mechanical engineer. If he had been he might have appreciated the practical problems in such a huge undertaking and never taken it on. As it was, Cox simply went to Scapa Flow, ignored the so-called experts who told him it was impossible and thought through the task for himself.

Cox was an extrovert genius who had a reckless disregard for any obstacles that got in the way of his quest. He purchased a giant German floating dock from the Admiralty and invested heavily to assemble the necessary equipment. Ironically the dock had been seized from Germany as part of the reparations demanded by the Allies as compensation for Reuter's scuttling of the Fleet. It could lift 3,000 tons and had previously been used by the Germans to lift U-boats. The dock was at that time one of the biggest ever built and was fitted out with pumps and compressors for dry-dock work.

Neither Cox nor the men he employed had any experience relevant to the work they were about to undertake but they threw themselves wholeheartedly into the task the experts had declared impossible. They found that the lighter destroyers had been scuttled two to three ships to one buoy and were lying virtually in heaps on the sea-bed with their masts and gear inextricably tangled together. The experts had taken the view that there was no lifting gear big enough to raise the far mightier battleships. Even if they could be raised by pumping compressed air into them, it was felt that they could not be kept on an even keel with the weight of their 12 to 15-inch gun-turrets bearing them down to one side or the other. Cox in characteristic fashion ignored them.

His first salvage attempt was the torpedo-boat destroyer V 70, an 800-ton vessel which lay on an even keel in about 15 metres of water. His floating dock was cut into two L-shaped sections which were manoeuvered into position on either side of the V 70's location. A lifting chain was passed under the propeller of the vessel from one L-shaped section to the other. This chain was tightened at low tide and as the tide subsequently turned, and the water level started to rise, it lifted the stern of the V 70 slightly off the bottom. The diving team could then get a second chain further under the keel and this was again tightened at low water. When the tide came in again the stern of the V 70 was lifted further off the bottom.

This process was repeated until there were eventually ten chains in position beneath the V 70, forming a cradle from end to end.

Finally Cox was ready to lift the V 70. Just before the tide was about to turn on a cold but bright morning in March 1924, Cox signalled to his 24 gangs of four winchmen apiece to make six turns on their winches. As the men wound, the docks began to tilt appreciably. Another six turns of the winch handles were ordered and his 96 winchmen strained at their task. After yet another six turns the men felt the V 70 start to lift. Suddenly there was an explosive bang from the vessel below the surface and the number ten chain whiplashed out of the water. Cox knew that the failure of one chain would fatally overload the nine remaining chains so he immediately ordered his winchmen to drop everything and hit the deck. As they did so, the other nine chains began to break in quick succession. Their half-hundredweight links whipped through the air. Some of the links broke free and hurtled over the heads of the terrified winchmen to impact on the metal deck-plates like shells. Cox himself narrowly missed a serious or indeed potentially fatal injury as a purchase block gyrated past him, its flailing end almost taking his head off. Mercifully no one was injured.

After this Cox learned by his mistakes and used 12 nine-inch 250-ton wire cables. These proved more reliable than chains and he was able to lift the V 70 successfully. The floating docks moved the V 70 into shallower water until she grounded. The whole process was repeated again and the V 70 was moved closer inshore. Eventually, six weeks later and after five such lifts in all, Cox was able to beach the V 70 on 4 August 1924. But once the V 70 broke the surface, Cox was furious to discover that everything that was removable, including her valuable torpedo tubes, had already been hacked off by locals. He threatened legal action if the culprits were to be discovered but the local community kept tight-lipped. Conveniently, no one could remember who had been involved and, needless to say, no one was ever held to account. Instead of having the V 70 broken down for scrap, Cox had her fitted out as a workshop.

Robertson had raised his four destroyers by the end of 1924 and carried out no further salvaging at Scapa Flow. Cox, however, continued with his own salvage effort, raising on average one vessel a month. Eleven days after the V 70 was raised, the S 53 was brought to the surface, followed by the S 55, the G 91, G 38 and S 52 all in the space of a few months.

In his first year he raised 18 vessels, averaging 750 tons each. By the summer of 1925 he had recovered half of his initial capital outlay of £45,000. He then purchased another even larger floating dock to mount an assault on the heavier destroyers that he had not been able to lift so far. With this dock he was able to raise all of the destroyers, with the last, the *G 104*, being raised on 1 May 1926.

The General Strike of that same year almost put paid to his salvage programme. The price of coal which he needed to run his boilers, pumps and compressors soared to more than £2 per ton. Financially, this was a ruinous price for him. He would be forced to close down within a matter of weeks. Having been presented with this problem Cox, in typical fashion, looked for a practical way to get round it. He remembered a diver had reported that the coal bunkers of the huge battle-cruiser were full. He immediately had teams of divers sent down on to the wreck to cut away the armoured plating above her bunkers. Once the bunkers were exposed he had the coal lifted out by mechanical grabs. He had discovered his own private coal supply and his boilers never went cold during the strike which crippled the rest of the country. The record for the fastest salvaged destroyer went to the *S 65*, which took only four days to recover. Cox sold the broken-down scrap for £50,000 and this helped to finance his assault on the biggest ships, the battle-cruisers or capital ships.

In 1926 he began work on the largest ship in the Fleet, the *Hindenburg*. If he could lift her she would be the largest ship ever salvaged. She was a massive vessel of 26,180 tons sitting on an even keel in about 21 metres of water. Her length at the water-line was 700 feet and her beam, 96 feet. Her distinctive tripod mast and twin funnels still stood proud of the water and her armament of eight massive 12-inch guns was still complete. His previous method for lifting the much lighter destroyers certainly would not manage to lift this monster for it had a greater displacement alone than the accumulated displacement of all 24 destroyers of the Fleet. It was decided to pump her dry where she lay.

Divers were sent down and began the laborious task of patching all the 800 holes, of varying size, in her hull by applying instant cement plugs. The diving teams had to work in appalling conditions. The work was done in the old style with Siebe-Gorman deep-sea diver's helmets and rubberised twill diving-suits. With lead boots, and weights on the diver's chest and back, the work was very arduous. It was made even more awkward by the continual misting over of the

front glass of the diver's helmet. The only way of getting round this was by using the spitcock, a short tube near the wearer's mouth leading from a valve on the outside of the helmet. The diver would put his mouth to the spitcock and, by opening the valve, draw in a mouthful of water. He would then shut the valve and spurt his mouthful of water over the front glass to clear the condensation. In teams of three, two divers would work below and the third would be fully kitted on standby on the surface in case of emergency. On the sea-bed the two divers were able to talk to each other by touching their helmets. A telephone system was soon installed but the use of the spitcock tended to short-out the connections. The divers found that seals inhabited the dark cabins and conger eels abounded in the pipes, torpedo tubes and, in particular, the engine-room workings. Working in darkness inside the hulls, the divers became familiar with their surroundings and learned to get around by touch, their heavy boots dragging in the mud and silt that layered the passages and cabins reducing what visibility there was to nil. The lead diver was followed by the second diver, whose job it was to see that his air hose and safety line did not become snagged on any protrusions.

After five months of this painstaking patching work the hull

The superstructure of the battle-cruiser *Hindenburg* as she rests on the bottom (IWM)

was nearly watertight. It was then discovered that the sealing patches were beginning to fail, letting water in. The local fish, saith, had found that the tallow used on the patches was very palatable and had been eating away at it. The failing patches were refitted with a less tasty mixture which had quick-setting cement in it and the ship was pumped dry.

When the first attempts were made to lift her she was found to list severely to one side and would have capsized had she not been allowed to sink back down on to the bottom again. Cox had one of the destroyers that he had raised previously grappled to the side of the *Hindenburg* to try to counter the list. From this destroyer he had a cable run to another salvaged destroyer which had been beached on the island of Cava about three-quarters of a mile away, to give a dead-weight as anchorage for the cable. The hull of the submerged vessel flooded during a gale but she was pumped dry once again. On 2 September 1926 she was successfully raised from the sea-bed. Shortly afterwards she flooded again and sank in another storm. After so many setbacks Cox gave up and abandoned her for the time being.

The focus of his salvage efforts was now the *Moltke*, another battle-cruiser of 22,640 tons sitting in 24 metres of water, upside-down and at an angle. Her water-line length was just over 610 feet and she had a beam of 96.5 feet. Her main armament was ten 11-inch guns, set in pairs, in five turrets of which three were on the centre line of the vessel. Again the procedure of plugging all the holes in the hull was gone through. On this vessel the work was much quicker and after a few weeks Cox was able to start pumping her dry where she lay. She began to lift slowly off the bottom, bow first. The bow proved to be the lighter end of the vessel. As it lifted so more and more air rushed to the higher bow, giving it even greater buoyancy. Divers monitoring the lift reported that the sealing patches were beginning to fail and the hull was starting to fill with water. Great bubbles of air began to belch from her starboard side. With this loss of buoyancy and the uneven distribution of the water in her, she started to list. If she were to capsize then, all the painstaking work of sealing the gaps where air could escape would be wiped out. With this in mind Cox decided to give up on the attempt and allowed her to settle on the bottom once more.

Cox decided to try another method. He had a special type of air-lock constructed from a line of old boilers which were welded together to form a huge pipe. This pipe was attached to the sunken hull of the *Moltke* and reached up to the

surface far above to form a connecting passageway from the surface to the hull. On the surface, the workers could enter the top of the tube by a hatch. They would find themselves in a small chamber which was then pressurised. Once the pressure in the chamber and the rest of the tube had been equalised another hatch could be opened at the bottom of the chamber and the workers could then climb down a ladder inside the huge pipe to the hull of the ship far below. Pumps were sent to the hull in this same fashion and compressed air was fed into one section of the hull by divers to create an air bubble. The salvagers could then go into the air bubble thus created and seal off the compartment that they were in to create a working environment. Every hole had to be sealed in this fashion, an extremely time-consuming task made even more difficult by the ship being upside-down. Floors and doors were far above their heads and staircases ran the wrong way. The salvagers had to erect scaffolding to get access to the connecting doors above them. Cox had learned from his earlier experiences of free air rushing to the part of the hull that lifted first. He had the hull sectioned off into three, sealed, airtight compartments. This would prevent the air becoming

Cox's innovative air-locks were still attached to the vessels as they were raised (OL)

40

Diver engaged on salvage operations (OL)

common and a repeat of the earlier problem. The sealing process took until May 1927 to complete.

The lifting effect of the compressed air was augmented by 20 nine-inch wire lifting cables which had been threaded under the hull. As with the *Hindenburg*, to counteract the list discovered in the earlier attempt to lift her, Cox used the colossal dead-weight of a water-filled, salvaged destroyer pontoon hung on her starboard side. Slowly Cox had the hull of the *Moltke* parbuckled to get her on to an even keel, albeit that she was still upside-down. The combined effect of the compressed air in the hull and the lifting cables managed to prise the *Moltke* free from the firm grip of the sea-bed. She began to rise slowly at first, breaking free from the suction of the mud. Once free she began to accelerate upwards like a cork. The air inside her expanded rapidly as the external pressure dropped and huge explosions of compressed air erupted from her, sending up six-metre waterspouts and clouds of vapour saturated with oil and coal dust. As the hull of the *Moltke* broke the surface of Scapa Flow for the first time in nine years, she achieved a delicate equilibrium and came to rest with about six metres of her upturned hull clear of the surface.

On 16 June 1927 Cox's tugs began to tow her to Lyness. On the way, the *Moltke* came abruptly to a sickening, yawing halt as one of her great guns hanging beneath her extended to full elevation and rammed its length into the hard sea-bed with all the weight of the *Moltke* following behind. Divers were sent down to blast the gun off her and the next day she was beached at Lyness. A standard-gauge railway was constructed from the shore on to the whale-back of the *Moltke's* hull by driving piles into the shore. On it, a light engine towed a three-ton crane-truck, enabling it to be used over any opening in the hull that was made. She was stripped of everything that could be removed where she lay. Much heavy machinery from the *Moltke* was cut up into sections and removed by using the crane. Two floating dock sections were moored beside the hull and on each deck ten-ton cranes were set up with jibs of extended reach. Also pressed into action was a 60-ton crane and end-lifting pulleys which could take up to 200 tons. In all about 3,000 tons of metal were stripped from her. Many artefacts were recovered in good condition from the hull and items such as clocks were found to be still capable of working and fetched good prices. After nine years' immersion inside the sunken vessel, bars of chocolate were recovered and found to be still edible. Bottles of wine in excellent condition were recovered from her, as were the brass band's musical instruments.

On 18 May 1927 the hull, still upside down, was taken in tow by three tugs which gave an aggregate of 6,000 horse-power. The tugs towed the *Moltke* down the east coast of Scotland for eventual breaking at Rosyth in the Firth of Forth, a journey of about 275 miles. The combined pulling power of the three tugs was enough to tow the *Moltke* at 3.5 mph. As preparations were being made for the long tow south her anchors were thrown. She strained at the moorings that held her to the floating dock. Suddenly there was a sharp crack as a steel hawser snapped. The gap between the dock and the *Moltke* began to widen and a gangway between them slipped, tilted and then dropped to hang vertically, held only at one side. A worker crossing it at the time had to cling to it like a monkey until it was caught by a crane. On the hazardous journey south 14 men were delegated to the job of keeping the *Moltke* afloat. They lived in one of two corrugated-iron huts that had been constructed on the hull. The other hut housed the pumps that were necessary to keep up the critical air

Bringing out the souvenirs from a salvaged vessel (OL)

pressure inside the hull. Despite all the effort that had been put into patching the air gaps in the hull, if the pumps were to be turned off or fail then the air would steadily find its way out of the hull. Correspondingly the hull would soon lose its buoyancy and sink.

As the *Moltke* approached the Firth of Forth disaster nearly struck. The tugs belonged to a German company that Cox had contracted to tow the hull south. Cox had already arranged for an Admiralty pilot to board the lead tug in the Firth of Forth to guide the hull in its final approach up the Firth to the naval dockyards at Rosyth. Unfortunately, he had neglected to tell the German contractors this and they, in the normal way, had engaged a civilian pilot to do just the same lucrative job. The two pilots came face-to-face on the tug and a bitter argument developed as to who had the right to guide the *Moltke* in. Both wanted to do it and neither was prepared to give way to the other. The argument went in circles and as they debated it escaped their notice that on the incoming tide the *Moltke* had actually started to make up ground on the tugs. The tow-lines went slack and, as she gathered her own momentum, the pilots realised that the lead tug was actually sailing past one side of the outcrop of rock in the middle of the Firth known as Inchcolm whilst the accelerating hulk of the *Moltke* was going past the other side. To avert certain disaster the crew had to cut away the towing cables as they began to catch on the islet. That immediate problem dealt with, it began to dawn on everyone concerned that the next obstacle in the path of the drifting 20,000 tons of German steel and armour plating was that great symbol of Victorian Scotland, the Forth Railway Bridge. The two pilots and crews looked on helplessly as the hulk drifted freely and completely out of control towards the great iron structure. A catastrophe seemed imminent. Thankfully, and much to the relief of the onlookers and no doubt the two pilots, the *Moltke* passed harmlessly through the gap between two immense legs of the bridge and disaster was averted. She was taken in tow again and led to the naval dockyard where she was subsequently broken up.

In 1928 Cox turned his attention to the *Seydlitz*, which lay in 21 metres of water on her side. She was practically a sister-ship to the *Moltke* with a water-line of 656 feet and a beam of 93 feet. About seven metres of her port side showed above the surface. The same method of patching and using air-locks was utilised but this time Cox was gambling on raising the hull as it lay on its side. The work proved laborious and fraught with difficulty. Time after time teams of divers were sent down into the murky, oily darkness to check on patches and look for the tell-tale stream of bubbles which would give away a leak. As she was being raised disaster struck. A forward patch failed and water started rushing into the hull. The weight of water caused one sealed-off, pressurised bulkhead after another to collapse and men working on her had to flee for their lives. The once isolated sealed sections now became one vast common air space as the compressed air expanded through the wrecked compartments, giving the bow more buoyancy than the stern. The great bow rose in the air. The centre of gravity of this 25,000-ton monster which had previously been finely adjusted was violently displaced and the *Seydlitz* rolled over sideways until her keel heaved up through the surface. Her bridgework and derrick posts struck the sea-bed and, with the impact, collapsed and stove in the decks above them, ruining the patches that had been fitted there. The air compressors fixed on the previously exposed hull were now submerged and useless. In a matter of seconds all the toil and effort of the last nine months was wiped out. To rub salt into the wound she had now settled in far deeper water. The indomitable Cox was furious but unbowed. He started the job all over again the next day.

Some 40 more test lifts and unsuccessful attempts were made to raise her from the bottom before the once-mighty vessel surrendered. While Cox was away on holiday his workers, in error, pumped too much compressed air into her hull and unexpectedly she lifted off the bottom and rose to the surface. When Cox learned of this he ordered that she be sunk immediately. He had already arranged with the world's media that the ship would be raised on 1 November in a blaze of publicity and he did not want to be robbed of his big moment! Surprisingly, after that, the lift on 1 November went off without any hitches.

For several months before the *Seydlitz* was raised Cox had men working on the 25,000-ton battleship *Kaiser* which lay capsized in 45 metres of water. Again workers used the air-lock system to get access to the submerged hull. Because the ship was so deep some of the air-locks were 12 to 18 metres tall. Inside the hull electric lighting was rigged up but, on going into the air-lock to climb the ladder to the surface, the men were plunged into darkness as soon as the lower hatch was closed. The long climb in darkness had to be done entirely by touch. As the climber neared the surface he would become aware of the howl of the storm and the tube would shudder as the sea pounded the air-lock. In the hull far below, the men were sheltered and cut off from conditions on the surface.

On 30 March 1929, after months of painstaking work, the *Kaiser* rose off the bottom, tight-sealed and with full buoyancy. Cox, as always thinking ahead to overcome any obstacles, had some time earlier made his workmen curious by having them fill an old boiler with concrete and set it on the sea-bed nearby. The deck plating round about the bridge was cut and weakened to the bemusement of his men. Once the *Kaiser* was up Cox had her towed, still in her upside-down position, until teams of divers reported that her conning-tower and superstructure were directly above the concrete-filled boiler. Cox then ordered that some compressed air be vented from the hull and it became clear what he was doing. The *Kaiser* slowly sank until the mass of her 25,000 tons was balanced on this one point. From far below, the onlookers heard the muffled sounds of metal being torn and bent. Within the submerged hull, deck after deck collapsed as the conning-tower section was forced up inside the hull. In this ingenious way Cox had managed to clear the conning-tower structure, which would have snagged as it was being towed for breaking, without losing it by having to cut or blast it free.

In May 1929 Cox turned his efforts to raising the fast mine-laying cruiser *Bremse* which lay capsized on the sea-bed with a heavy list. After the scuttling had started, a British boarding party had taken her in tow and made for the nearest land in a race against time to beach her before she sank. They almost succeeded. She had run her bows aground and then rolled over. As a result of the shelving of the sea-bed her bows were high and dry but her stern was under almost 20 metres of water. Cox had her sealed off into watertight compartments where she lay and by the end of July she was at a pitch of negative buoyancy and ready to be lifted. Diving teams cut and blasted away her bridge superstructure to avoid any snagging when she was in tow. By fixing an array of nine-inch cables to the lower side of the hull and linking these to the two largest docks, Cox arranged the method of parbuckling her to get her on to an even keel. The cables were wound in at low tide and as the tide subsequently rose the cables turned her over. Once she had been brought upright the hull was brought to full buoyancy and, inch by inch, she was brought to the surface over a period of two days and then taken to Lyness for breaking.

In 1930 Cox decided to have another attempt to realise his burning ambition of lifting the *Hindenburg* and achieving the greatest feat of marine salvage ever. This was the ship that he dreamed about lifting and yet it was the one that had thwarted all his earlier attempts. Divers surveyed the ship and reported that some 500 out of the original 800 patches were intact. The others had to be repaired or renewed by teams of divers working round the clock. The experience Cox had gained since his earlier attempts to lift her now stood him in good stead. Once pumping was under way she began to rise off the sea-bed majestically. When her upperworks had risen almost five metres clear of the water, a sudden anxiety showed across the faces of the onlookers as

The superstructure of the salvaged *Hindenburg* although her decks are still awash (OL)

she began to roll over under the weight of the water that was still swilling about inside her. Cox ordered that the air pressure inside her be reduced and she was allowed to settle back down on the sea-bed.

Later another attempt was made to raise her. Again she came up dead level at first and then, once more, began to roll. She developed a list of $2°$ and the tension began to mount as the readings were called out . . . $2\frac{1}{2}°$ then steadily on to $3°$, $3\frac{1}{2}°$, $4°$, $4\frac{1}{2}°$, $5°$, $5\frac{1}{2}°$, $6°$, $6\frac{1}{2}°$ and then there was silence. Suddenly the cry went out that the list had decreased to $6°$, then $5\frac{1}{2}°$ and then $5°$. She was now steadily righting herself. She smoothly rolled back until she was on an even keel and stopped dead level. The pumping continued and more and more of the great ship revealed herself.

Once the decks were at the surface, even though they were still awash, Cox jumped down on to her from the floating dock. A workman decided to follow and share in Cox's great moment. He too jumped from the dock on to the deck but unfortunately he chose a part of the deck where there was a cavity and promptly vanished. Then his soaked head appeared and he cried out for help because he could not swim. Cox, in a rare show of playfulness, hauled him out and then, grinning from ear to ear, gave him a piggy-back back towards the dockside. On their way back, to the amusement of the crowds of workmen who had come to watch this comedy, Cox stumbled and the two of them went headlong into the water and vanished again, only to reappear seconds later, clinging to each other and laughing wildly. After all the years of set-back and toil it was a rare moment of levity. It was 23 July 1930.

Next on the agenda was the 19,500-ton battle-cruiser *Von der Tann*. She lay capsized with a $17\frac{1}{2}°$ list, with the water depth over her ranging from seven to 12 metres. She was sectioned off and made watertight. A few test lifts of the bow and stern were carried out to make sure that the final lift would go smoothly. During the sealing-off process three workers had a narrow escape whilst cutting through some pipework with oxy-acetylene cutters inside the submerged hull. The flame ignited a pocket of trapped gas and there was a large explosion which badly damaged the compartment they were working in and injured all three. Water started rushing in. The explosion had blown out all the lights and in the darkness they discovered, to their horror, that the way out of the cabin was now blocked by a blown-out section of bulkhead. The rush of water into the cabin continued unabated and the terrified men were painfully aware that a horrible death in the cold water and darkness of their submerged tomb awaited them. They clambered up to the highest point in the cabin, trying to keep their heads above the relentlessly rising water. The water rose as far as their chins and then miraculously the sound of the rushing water stopped. An air bubble had been formed and for the time being the immediate prospect of death receded. The cabin was silent but the men knew that they had only bought time and that they would soon use up the precious air.

As soon as the explosion occurred, the other men working in the vicinity made their way towards the area where the three had been working. From the deck space above they found that all the surrounding cabins had filled with sea-water and their first thoughts were that the cabin in which the three had been working must be flooded too and the three dead. They could not hear the trapped men's frantic cries for help through the thick armoured deck, although the trapped men could hear their rescuers above tapping with hammers on the deck in the hope of getting a response. They had nothing with which they could signal their presence in return. The rescuers squatted on the deck fearing the worst because

Pumping the
Hindenburg dry
(OL)

of the lack of a response. As they waited for a diver to arrive to go down into the flooded deck, one rescuer, to his astonishment, saw a hose connection which led from beneath the blocked cabin doorway move. He knew at once that the men were alive and trying to signal their presence. The rescuers then took a tremendous all-or-nothing gamble with their own lives to free them, knowing that they would not have much air left in the flooded cabin. Risking another gas explosion, they used an oxy-acetylene cutter and cut through to the cabin below. Once the cutting had started the trapped air bubble was able to filter out through the cut and the water level in the cabin began to rise again. One by one they were able to grab hold of the outstretched hands and pluck the men to safety.

By the time that Cox finally raised the *Von der Tann* the price of scrap metal had crashed and to have broken her would have ruined them. He therefore focused his efforts on lifting his last ship, the *Prinzregent Luitpold*, in the hope that in the six months that it would take to raise her the scrap metal price would improve. During the preparations for lifting her, an explosion in the submerged hull blew in a bulkhead and killed one of the workers. The other men working inside had to flee from the smoke and water that rapidly filled the hull.

By 1933 the scrap metal price had picked up and Cox had the *Von der Tann* and *Prinzregent Luitpold* towed to Rosyth for breaking. At the end of his eight years of salvage work at Scapa Flow he was £10,000 down.

The Alloa Shipbreaking Company (later known as Metal Industries) now took over the job of salvaging the remnants of the High Seas Fleet and did so more successfully than Cox. They were able to generate a profit of about £50,000 on each of the larger ships they raised. In June 1933 the 28,000-ton *Bayern* was raised from the sea-bed spectacularly. A blow-out in a compressed air pipe caused too much air to be fed into the ship. She lifted off the sea-bed slowly at first but as soon as she broke free from its muddy grip she shot upwards like a cork, reaching the surface in only 30 seconds.

The lifts were now becoming more practised and the *Grosser Kurfürst* soon saw the light of day again, followed by the *Kaiserin* in May 1936 and the *Friedrich der Grosse* in April 1937. In 1939 the last of the battle-cruisers, the 26,180-ton *Derfflinger*, was raised from the record depth of 45 metres. She was taken to Rosyth for breaking but as the war clouds over Europe darkened and the world watched Hitler's military build-up apprehensively, the Admiralty retook control of the dry dock where all the breaking of the salvaged vessels had been carried out. The *Derfflinger* therefore remained afloat awaiting her final fate throughout the war until finally being taken apart in 1946. She was the last of the High Seas Fleet to be salvaged whole.

During the succeeding years the remaining wrecks were left to lie in peace, until Nundy (Marine Metals) Ltd, run by Arthur Nundy, an ex-Metal Industries diver realised the value of the non-ferrous metals still in them. Holes were blasted in the two battleships, *König* and *Kronprinz Wilhelm*, around the engine and boiler room areas and the magazines and torpedo rooms to allow access for salvage divers. Other smaller salvage companies followed this practice and most of the remaining wrecks bear the scars of this smaller scale salvage work around their engine and boiler room areas.

The remnants of the scuttled German High Seas Fleet could not economically be salvaged today in their present condition. Many people have considered it carefully but, structurally, after 70 years' immersion in corrosive salt water and the blasting that has been carried out on them, they are no longer sound and even for Cox the feat would have been impossible.

Since the advent of the nuclear age in 1945 the surrounding environment has had a higher level of radioactivity. The relatively radiation-free steel used to construct the Fleet in those pre-Hiroshima days has now acquired a higher value than just its basic scrap value. There is a dwindling supply of radiation-free steel in the world today. What little supplies there are are literally just rusting away. All steel manufactured today has a higher radiation level. The earlier metal is needed for delicate instruments that measure radioactivity itself and in the protective shielding for medical instruments that use certain set levels of radiation. Systematically over more recent times, parts of the remaining ships have been blasted off and taken to the surface, destroying the structural integrity of the ships. Every now and then you will come across a gaping hole where a chunk has been blown off. I am sure that no diver will have any regrets that they cannot be lifted. They will remain where they are to provide spectacular and exciting diving for many years to come.

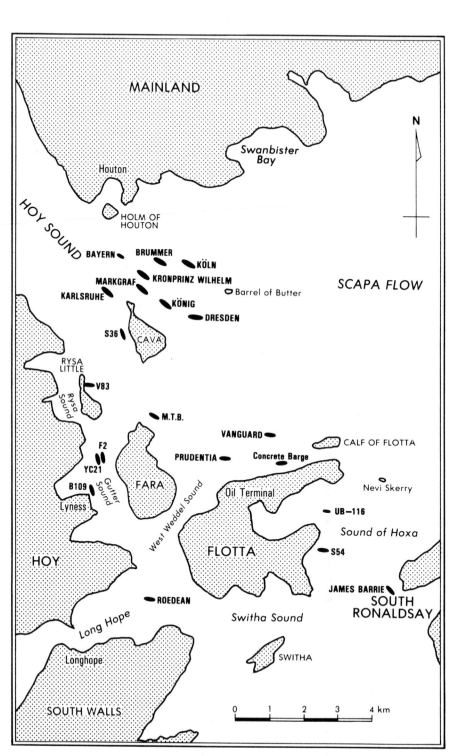

MAINLAND

Swanbister Bay

Houton

HOY SOUND

HOLM OF HOUTON

BAYERN   BRUMMER
                        KÖLN
MARKGRAF   KRONPRINZ WILHELM   SCAPA FLOW
KARLSRUHE   Barrel of Butter
                    KÖNIG
            S36   DRESDEN
                CAVA

RYSA LITTLE
        V83
Rysa Sound

            M.T.B.
                VANGUARD   CALF OF FLOTTA
        F2   PRUDENTIA   Concrete Barge
        YC21
    B109   Oil Terminal   Nevi Skerry
    Lyness Gutter Sound FARA   West Weddel Sound
                            UB—116
HOY   Sound of Hoxa
                    FLOTTA   S54

                    JAMES BARRIE
            ROEDEAN   SOUTH RONALDSAY
    Long Hope   Switha Sound

    Longhope   SWITHA

SOUTH WALLS   0   1   2   3   4 km

Existing wreck sites

Diving the Scuttled German High Seas Fleet Today

Today, only a fraction of the High Seas Fleet's original might is left in the depths of Scapa Flow for sports divers to explore. But coupled with the countless other wrecks in this area, they make for one of the world's most prolific wreck sites. Scapa Flow is fast becoming a Mecca for divers. Many groups now come from Europe and the USA to experience this great attraction.

The High Seas Fleet

Three 26,000-ton battleships, *König*, *Kronprinz Wilhelm* and *Markgraf*, and four 4,000 to 5,000-ton light cruisers, *Brummer*, *Dresden*, *Köln* and *Karlsruhe*, still lie on the sea-bed where they settled after their journey from the surface along with torpedo-boat destroyers, the four great 600-ton gun-turrets of the *Bayern*, a First World War U-boat, *UB-116*, and innumerable other vessels that have for various reasons ended their lives in this natural harbour since then.

The battleships

The three battleships, *König*, *Kronprinz Wilhelm* and *Markgraf*, are immense. They each displaced 25,388 tons at the time of their launch and the colossal weight of their fighting decks and gun-turrets caused them to turn turtle as they sank so that they now lie with their huge whale-back hulls upwards. A dive on one of these giants will only scratch the surface of it. You could spend a whole week diving on a single battleship before you would really get to know it. In their time they were the state of the art in warship construction: 'dreadnoughts' that had for the first time in centuries threatened Britain's traditional naval supremacy.

Britain has the good fortune to be an island and this natural feature meant that at that time, as long as a strong navy was maintained, the British Isles need have little fear of being invaded. Invasion would only have been possible from the sea. This premise had led to the development of the 'two-power standard' that was to govern the Royal Navy's thinking for many years. The principle was that the Royal Navy must always be equal in strength to the combined sea-power of the second and third most powerful navies in the world. At the end of the 19th century Kaiser Wilhelm II and the then Captain Alfred von Tirpitz had masterminded the creation of a huge German naval build-up much to the alarm of the British, whose powerful navy was weakened by being spread all over the world to meet its global commitments.

In the run-up to the First World War, Germany and Britain had become locked in a naval arms race that was to lead to the creation of the dreadnought as each side vied for naval supremacy. The dreadnoughts were so far advanced technologically that they made the 'pre-dreadnoughts' obsolete practically overnight. Britain led the way with the construction in 1906 of the battleship HMS *Dreadnought* which was to give its name to the class of ships that followed it.

The new dreadnoughts were about ten per cent bigger and cost at that time £1.75 million. These revolutionary battleships were equipped with ten 12-inch guns, each of which could fire a 850-lb shell 18,500 yards. Three of the five gun-turrets were centred on the middle line of the vessel with one gun-turret on either side amidships. It could therefore fire a broadside of eight shells to either side, six ahead and two astern. One dreadnought could match two pre-dreadnoughts for firepower at long range and three when firing ahead.

Before the dreadnought era battleships had had no centralised fire control. Each gun was fired independently of the others. The dreadnoughts had the latest in range-finding techniques, sighting and fire control. All eight guns were for the first time aimed and fired by one gunnery officer positioned in an observation nest halfway up the foremast. The dreadnoughts also had the latest 11-inch armour and faster new engines. They were indeed a revolution in naval warfare.

The light cruisers
The four light cruisers, *Brummer*, *Dresden*, *Köln* and *Karlsruhe*, are quite considerably smaller, weighing in at between 4,400 tons and 5,600 tons. Nevertheless these wrecks are still large vessels which provide spectacular and exciting diving. With the exception of the *Karlsruhe* they are in better condition than the inverted battleships. They lie on their side and are more recognisable for what they are. They are more

accessible and are considered by many to be better dives. There are so many features still instantly recognisable on these ships that they are fascinating to dive. Swimming over these light cruisers today you can picture what they would have been like in their heyday.

Dropping down the shot-line to the bow of the *Köln* it is easy to orientate yourself on her as she lies on her side. Peering over the bulwark rail and down her now vertical deck, the area below looks black and it is at first difficult to pick out any features. There is a marked contrast between the sunlit hull and the deck which is in the shadow of the hull. To drift over and down the deck is like crossing to the dark side of the moon. As you drop over the side your eyes adjust to the darkness as you regulate your buoyancy. The sharp pointed form of the bow itself takes shape. Swimming away from the bow towards the stern you come across the anchor chains dropping the run out from the chain lockers to the capstans and from there dropping into the darkness beneath you to the sea-bed. The original wooden deck planking can still be seen. Finning further back you come across the remnants of where the 5.9-inch gun-turrets have been removed and then jutting outwards from the deck at right angles looms the armoured bridge with its thin viewing slits ringing its circular structure. Above it there is a smaller armoured viewing deck with similar slits and a large winged device, the central gun-control range-finder, situated on top. Floating beyond the bridge, the foremast looms up with its searchlight platforms still easily recognisable. Further back yet to the area where the triple funnels once stood, empty lifeboat davits hang out, a silent reminder of the actual scuttling itself when the lifeboats were lowered as the vessel sank into the water. Just aft of them a 5.9 inch gun, still in its protective turret, juts upward at an awkward angle above the mainmast towards the distant surface of the sea. Further on, the hull, with its rows of portholes, stops abruptly where salvagers have blasted a cavernous hole 12 metres wide. Immediately to your left you will see the mainmast running off into the darkness with its searchlight platform still in place. Float over the tangled wreckage barely discernible below, and at the limit of your visibility the hull seems to take shape again. You are getting near the stern now and suddenly the breach mechanism and turret of one of her upper deck 5.9-inch guns appears. After pausing to inspect the encrusted workings swim on along the gun barrel. Pressing on as time is getting short you come to the now horizontal drop to the main deck where another 5.9-inch gun turret dominates with an anchor capstan visible under its raised barrel. At last you are at the stern, which is covered with sponges and sea anemones but sadly it is time to return to the surface. As you drift slowly upwards the shape of the *Köln* begins to blur and then get fainter below you until finally it merges with the background. What a dive! You have only skimmed over her so the next time you dive her you can take your time to inspect a section of her in more detail.

Bye-laws

Today, diving in Scapa Flow is governed by the Orkney Harbour Areas Bye-Laws 1977 which regulate the safe and continuous movement of shipping in this section of the harbour. Copies can be obtained from the Department of Harbours at the Harbour Authority Building at Scapa and it is from this same department that the mandatory diving permits are issued. If you are diving with one of the boat charterers then the permits will automatically be obtained for you. The terms of the permit are important and are worth repeating:

3. The person or persons to whom this permit is granted has permission to dive upon the wrecks of the *Brummer, Dresden,* and *Köln* only, being wrecks in the ownership of Orkney Islands Council. The owner's permission must be obtained before any other individual wrecks are dived upon.

4. (a) No part or artefacts of any wreck may be removed without the prior written permission of the owner of the wreck. Any part or artefacts removed must be declared to HM Customs & Excise, the Receiver of Wreck.

(b) With reference to the wrecks of the *Brummer, Dresden* and *Köln*, it should be noted that (i) the granting of this permit in no way implies permission to remove any parts or artefacts from these wrecks and separate application must be made for any such permission, and (ii) all fittings which in the opinion of the Ministry of Defence are of a confidential character and any cash, notes, securities for money, books or personal effects remain in the control of the Ministry of Defence and persons are strictly prohibited from removing any such items. Any person locating any such items shall notify the Department of Harbours so that a report can be made to the Ministry of Defence.

5. The wreck of HMS *Royal Oak* and the wreckage of HMS *Vanguard* are designated 'war graves' and it is not the policy of the Ministry of Defence (Navy) to permit diving on such vessels. Paragraph 33 of the Orkney Islands Council General Bye-Laws prohibits diving within 100 metres of any of Her Majesty's ships or vessels including the wrecks of any such ships or vessels.

6. No person or persons shall dive within 500 metres of the Flotta Terminal, the Single Point Moorings and all submarine pipelines

associated with the developments on the island of Flotta or the Single Point Moorings (details of which are available from the undersigned).

7. This permission is granted on condition that neither the Orkney Islands Council nor any of its servants or agents shall be liable to any person for any loss or damage of any kind howsoever caused or arising from the use of this Diving Permit or arising by virtue of Orkney Islands Council's ownership of the wrecks of the *Brummer*, *Dresden* and *Köln* and the person or persons to whom the permission is granted shall relieve and indemnify Orkney Islands Council from and against all loss, damage, responsibility, liability, claims and expenses which may be sustained or incurred by or made upon or against them on account of or by or through the said use or failure to comply with the conditions of this permit.

8. The person in charge of the craft used for the purpose of the permit shall ensure that the Diving Flag—International Code Flag 'A'—is flown at all times when divers are in the water.

Depute Director of Harbours, Orkney Islands Council, Scapa.

Visibility

Generally the visibility in Scapa Flow is very good, averaging about ten to 15 metres. In the crisp early months of the year the visibility can be much better but then only the keenest of divers would venture into the water in Orkney and be able to tell the tale. The weather would seldom permit diving and the biting wind creates a severe wind chill factor. Beware, however, when planning a diving trip, of the 'plankton bloom' which generally occurs twice a year, in late May and September. The times do fluctuate from year to year and it would be wise to check on this when you book your holiday and take advice from the men who sail these waters as their living. The 'plankton bloom' will severely decrease your visibility and ruin your holiday. From having good visibility of ten to 15 metres you can end up with visibility of less than five.

Sea-bed

The sea-bed in the Flow itself is generally a silty mixture and is easily stirred up so try to keep above it to avoid spoiling the visibility for the rest of your party. Do not make any attempt to go inside the wrecks no matter how inviting a passageway or dark hole may look. Only experienced divers, properly equipped with ropes and the like, should even attempt it. Fine silt layers the corridors inside and is easily stirred up. Careless finning in a confined space can quickly reduce the visibility to nil. Once that happens you won't know which way you came in and will soon become totally disorientated. Finding your way out may be impossible and at 30 metres plus down you won't have long on your air supply to get out. One of my buddies discovered this the hard way (see the section on the *Köln*). Don't make the mistake he did. There have been a number of well-publicised diving tragedies at Scapa Flow over the last few years. They are nearly all caused by divers penetrating the wrecks or by excessive repeat diving. Sadly they are nearly all preventable. Keep a careful watch of your contents gauge. The German Fleet is deep and you will be amazed at how quickly your air supply will be used up. You can almost watch the needle falling as you swim over these great ships! It is not just a symptom of the nitrogen narcosis that you will inevitably (and perhaps unknowingly) be experiencing at that depth!

Weather
The weather conditions at Scapa Flow range from extremes and can change quickly. On some occasions I have dived, conditions have been ideal. No wind, a fierce sun beating down and the surface of the water still and glistening with an oily shimmer like a mill pond. On other occasions (often the following day!) the dive-boat has been tossed around contemptuously like a cork, a biting northerly wind has been blowing and the period in between dives has been most unpleasant—in effect a continual battle to keep warm and out of the wind. There are no hard and fast rules. Scapa Flow is temperamental and it really is a case of paying your money and taking your chance.

The diving season at Scapa Flow runs from March through to October and you can nearly always be guaranteed diving somewhere in the Flow no matter which way the wind is blowing. As Scapa Flow is nearly completely enclosed by land you will always find a lee giving a dive site. If the wind is blowing from the north-west then the westerly Barrier wrecks may be undiveable because of surface conditions. By just crossing the six metres of the Barrier to the easterly side you will find that the sea is calm and the wrecks diveable.

The dive-boats are robust vessels, often old fishing boats which can cope with the worst that can be thrown at them inside the relatively protected enclaves of the Flow. It will really be up to the dive-marshall in charge of the particular dive-group to determine what is sensible. The surface of the Flow can be extremely rough but with little current in the Flow itself, as soon as you are under the water the surface problems disappear. It is only on surfacing that any difficulty will arise. In a heavy sea the dive-boat will roll quite markedly.

As you approach the boat the skipper will shield you with the boat from the worst of the weather but it is once you grab hold of the vertical steel ladder up the side of the boat that your problems will begin. One minute you can have your feet on the rungs and be largely submerged. The next, with the roll of the boat, you can find that you are lifted virtually entirely out of the water without having moved your feet. It is a slow and acrobatic climb up the ladder but then, once at the top, you have to time your final step and swing into the boat to coincide with the boat rolling the right way. Otherwise you may loose your balance and be pitched backwards into the sea to the amusement of those on board.

As a general rule April can be very stormy although as compensation there are fewer divers about. From May to August the conditions are generally good and then worsen through September with the diving really ending in October, by which time it can be very stormy.

If you are going out on the water on one of those typically windy days remember to take a woollen hat for your head. It may not be 'macho' but I cannot over-emphasise how biting the wind can be. If your head is wet after your first dive the wind chill will soon be gnawing at your very bones. You will almost certainly get a head cold which will prevent you diving and ruin your stay in Orkney.

Equipment

Most divers visiting Orkney have dry or semi-dry suits and in my opinion they are essential for deep repeat diving such as this. The first time I visited Scapa was relatively early in the diving calendar. It was May and although on the surface the conditions were great, the water had not yet warmed up at all, or so it felt. I dived every day in my trusty old wet suit. It had served me well for many years diving locally around Aberdeenshire's coast and on the west coast of Scotland but had never been faced with a challenge like Scapa Flow. Above the water the sun was beating down and initially it was a relief to enter the cool of the water. Once down on the German wrecks I very soon found the cold a problem. A neoprene diving suit is compressed considerably by the water pressure at 35 metres and loses much of its insulative quality. Shivering through a dive takes the pleasure away from it. Once back on the surface my buddy and I could only laugh uncontrollably as we both tried to pour soup from a flask into our cups. We were both shivering and shaking so much that we couldn't get much in successfully and what we did was spilled all over the deck as we raised the cups to our mouths. It is of course a purely personal view but I have used a dry suit ever since. It is easier to pull on a warm and dry suit when you are warm and dry than to have to struggle with numb hands with a cold, wet, wet suit. I still meet some wet-suited divers at Scapa who insist that they do not feel the cold. I applaud them but at the same time wonder how much is the truth and how much is bravado.

A good torch is essential. Even although you will not be going inside the wrecks themselves there are many openings to peer into that will give you an insight into the innards of the vessels. It is not so dark that you will need a torch to see your way around, although at 35 metres it is gloomy. As a diver descends, the effect of the water is progressively to filter out all the red colours so that at the depth of the German wrecks no real colours stand out. A torch will help you identify objects by showing their true colours and is also useful for signalling to your buddy in the gloom.

Photography
Photography on the deeper German wrecks can be difficult. At 35 to 45 metres to the sea-bed they are so deep that there is little natural light around and it is necessary to rely on your flash to photograph objects close to you. By using natural light only and a long exposure you can get some good photographs of larger sections of the ships but conditions have to be right. Your flash will only travel about six feet at this depth and what seemed like a great shot when it was taken can be disappointing when developed. Beyond the effective range of the flash will appear completely dark. It is, sadly, a false and inaccurate reflection of what it is like down on the German Fleet. The taker of the photograph can probably see for about 12 metres and sees a completely different picture.

Photography on the shallower wrecks however can be very successful. The water around the blockships on the western side of the Churchill Barriers has a considerable amount of silt particles suspended in it, clouding the water and making photography a test of skill. The seaward easterly Barrier wrecks are much better. Best of all are the Burra Sound blockships, *Inverlane, Gobernador Bories, Doyle* and *Tabarka*. The visibility in Burra Sound is far better than anything in the Flow and it is not uncommon to get 20 to 25 metres crystal-clear visibility. The silt is swept away by the fierce tidal rip through the Sound so there are considerably fewer particles to reflect your flash back at you and spoil a good picture. The Burra Sound wrecks have far more natural light which means that beyond the range of your flash the lens will pick up the surrounding background for some distance, adding reality and perspective to the photograph. The fish are plentiful and friendly and accustomed to being fed by hand. Entire sections of plating are covered with a rich profusion of sponges and anemones. If photography is your passion then head for the Burra Sound blockships. You will not be disappointed.

Decompression
Most of the divers coming to Scapa Flow today come for a minimum of one week's diving. With all the scuttled German Fleet wrecks to explore and the countless other wrecks and dive-sites, it is easy to see why divers who have been to the Flow tend to come back time and time again. Friendly relationships are struck up with the dive-boat operators who will take pains to accommodate each group's diving wishes as much as possible. The abundance of first class dive sites, allied to the distance and cost involved in getting to Scapa Flow, leads to an understandable tendency to try to cram as much diving as possible into the available time. This in itself can lead to problems of fatigue, residual nitrogen build-up and the like. Two dives a day is the norm but the dive-boat skippers stress that they have no control over what diving is done from their boats. They will leave the details of the diving to the party's dive-marshall, subject of course to their overriding veto if the prevailing weather conditions are bad. If the dive party wants to dive three or more times a day then the dive-boat charterer will comply with that. Repeat diving to this level should not be encouraged. The diving is deep and arduous. Each dive will sap your body's strength and stamina. A lot of nitrogen is absorbed by the body each time and even though you may be observing decompression tables to the full, a residual level of nitrogen will be carried over from one dive to the next. The amount varies from person to person depending on his physical make-up. It is unfortunately all too common to hear of divers getting bent doing regular repeat dives whilst diving within the tables. As a safety precaution divers should consider having a day's break or even a half-day's break halfway through the week to allow the body to get rid of any residual nitrogen build-up. Some of the skippers will actually encourage dive-parties to take such a break but again they are subject to the wishes of the dive group that has chartered their boat and will not enforce such a break if it is not wanted.

Until a few years ago it was common to have only two dives in any one day with the odd dive such as a night dive as the exception. The dives would be separated by a six-hour decompression gap. With the advent of the new decompression tables and the dive computer there is now the potential to dive longer and more often. Three or more dives in any one day is becoming increasingly common in Scapa Flow. As a matter of pure common sense it does not pay to push your diving too hard in the one week that you find yourself in Orkney. Most divers will not have dived as regularly and as deep as this. Your body will not have been prepared for the stresses and strains of a week's deep repeat diving. Many divers coming to Scapa Flow will not be fully dive fit. They may not dive regularly with their own club or may not be used to diving at this depth; also, they may be taking medication incompatible with diving. Late nights spent discussing the day's diving highlights and sipping the local brew, whilst sometimes as good as the diving, all add to the strain on the body, weakening it and making it more susceptible to decompression problems. There is no doubt about it. A week's diving in Scapa Flow is hard work but, if done sensibly, will give you some of the best diving in the world.

Dive-boat charterers
Diving is mainly done from hard boats, often old fishing boats. There are about ten dive-boat charterers working in Scapa Flow at the moment. Full details can be found in chapter eight. Some are based in Stromness where the ferry from Scrabster on the mainland comes in. Others are based in Kirkwall or the easterly islands of the Churchill Barriers, such as Burray and South Ronaldsay. Some are flexible and will pick up divers from whichever town they are staying. There are a variety of dive-packages on offer. Some offer an all-in deal with accommodation on board their boats in bunks and cabins. Once the day's diving is over the skipper will anchor somewhere to let the divers ashore to get some food and drink before returning to the boat for the night. Others will arrange accommodation throughout Orkney to suit varying tastes and budgets. All the dive-boats have compressors on board and some have additional shore-based back-up compressors. All will be able to provide bottles and weights if required. Some include these in the total package cost but others will make a small additional charge. It would be a wise precaution to take your own backpack and weight-belt if you intend hiring bottles and weights there because not all the operators have them included or available. Alternatively, check in advance to see exactly what is provided. There is no commercial dive-shop in Orkney to help you out in your time of need although there is a

sports shop in Kirkwall that sells a limited selection of diving accessories. It would also be wise to book your week's diving at Scapa Flow well in advance. Diving is becoming very popular in Orkney and there is now some competition to get the most sought-after weeks. It is common to find clubs booking their following year's diving at the end of their week in Scapa Flow to ensure that they get the week they want.

Diving practice
The dive party normally assembles at between eight and nine in the morning, depending on how keen everyone is. Once all the divers and their gear are aboard, the dive-boat will set off towards the first site. The journey out from Stromness or Burray to the deeper German wrecks will take about an hour, depending on weather conditions. Once on-site the skipper will probably drop a buoyed shot-line on to the wreck but will not anchor above the wreck. The wrecks are so big that it would seriously impinge on your available bottom time if you had to cut short your dive halfway through to return to the shot-line to ascend. The average depth of the High Seas Fleet wrecks is 35 to 45 metres so your non-stop bottom time is short enough anyway. The common practice therefore is to surface in the normal way without trying to find your way back to the shot-line. The skipper will be able to collect you as you surface. The surfacing and pick-up drills should be agreed with the skipper beforehand. If your skipper does drop a shot on to one of the wrecks do not use it as a means of hauling yourself down. Use it more as a guide to ensure you hit the wreck. There is little current in the middle of the Flow where the wrecks lie. The battleships sit upside down with their whale-back hulls facing upwards, presenting a relatively smooth surface with little to snag the shot. If you haul at the shot-line as you go down you may well find that you have pulled the shot off the hull and that you miss the top of the hull, or indeed the wreck itself, and find yourself dropping straight down to the sea-bed at 45 metres.

After the first dive has been completed the skipper will be able to take you ashore to let you get some food and perhaps do a bit of sightseeing on one of the neighbouring islands. The old naval base of Lyness, on the nearby island of Hoy, is very popular with dive-boats and it is not uncommon to find a number of them tied up over lunch and the one pub on the island that does bar meals absolutely packed with divers. After eating you can visit the nearby naval museum which has a number of interesting exhibits on display, including the huge bronze prop and wood-lined drive shaft of the *Hampshire*. The naval cemetery lies nearby and the graves of the nine German sailors who were killed on the day of the scuttling can be seen, along with the graves of British sailors who lost their lives in the two world wars, including those of the *Royal Oak* and *Vanguard*. Set at a tangent to the rest of the graves are the graves of some Muslim sailors facing Mecca. High on the hill that overlooks Lyness can be seen the large fortified building that was the Allies' HQ for their Atlantic operations during the two wars.

Provided the decompression tables permit it, a second dive can be carried out later in the day on the German wrecks or, alternatively, on the many good shallower wrecks such as the blockships or the *F 2* which lies just outside Lyness. The blockships make very good second dives or night dives.

Once the last dive of the day has been finished the skipper will take you back to your base if you are staying ashore. If you are staying on board then he will moor somewhere suitable to let you ashore to enjoy the local food and amber nectar before flopping exhausted into your bunk.

Diving from inflatables
It is possible to dive Scapa Flow from an inflatable, although you will have to know your stuff to find the German wrecks, as generally they are not buoyed. The wrecks are marked on the Admiralty charts for the area but you will need a good compass and an echo-sounder or magnetometer to find them. You will know instantly when you are over them because of their sheer size. The bottom of the Flow is generally flat and undulating with no real features to confuse with the wrecks. The echo-sounder will be showing the bottom at 35 to 45 metres and then suddenly the line will jump straight up to 15 to 20 metres. Although Scapa Flow is a natural harbour it is many miles wide and in this expanse of water it is easy to misjudge distance and miss them if you don't have the right equipment. In the busier months you will find that there will often be one or more dive-boats with divers down on site so that will give you an idea of the location. Many of the blockships have parts of their superstructure visible above the water and so are no problem to get on to. In fact some of the best diving around Scapa Flow is to be found on the *Inverlane*, *Tabarka*, *Doyle* and *Gobernador Bories* in Burra Sound. The bows of the *Inverlane* jut high out of the water and can easily be recognised, on your right, from the mainland ferry on your approach to Stromness. Although these wrecks can only be dived at slack water it is worth the effort. The fierce current

that runs through this Sound has scoured the sea-bed of any sand or silt and so the visibility here is excellent, averaging 20 to 25 metres. The wrecks teem with fish that have become so used to divers thrusting tasty morsels at them that large fish, such as the normally timid wrasse, will now spot a diver and positively demand to be fed. The fish will follow divers over the wreck on the off-chance of getting fed.

Overall, it is much more convenient and probably as cheap in the long run for a group to charter one of the local dive-boats. If you do decide to go it alone you will find that the cost of taking your inflatable on a trailer across in the ferry is quite expensive. You will be charged for your car, the passengers in it and will have to pay about the same again for your boat. If you are going in a group it will be just as cheap to take one of the dive-packages and I thoroughly recommend this as the way to dive Scapa Flow. Your skipper will ensure that you get a great week's diving and that there are no ill-fated and depressing attempts to dive the wrecks that end up with nothing but a dive on a flat, featureless and uninteresting silty bottom and a resultant red face! If you cannot get a large enough group together do not despair—12 is the maximum number of divers for any one dive-boat in the Flow. If you have a smaller group it may be possible for a charterer to double you up with a similar small group to fill the dive-boat or do a special cheaper deal if you are going at one of the quieter times of the year. From May through to October, however, they are normally fully booked but it is still worth while enquiring.

If you do decide to take an inflatable, there is no point in working out of Stromness or Burray. You will have the same lengthy journey to and from the dive sites. It is one thing to have to spend the journey out in a large, comfortable, heated hard boat, getting kitted up in the luxury of a heated changing room. It is another story to have a 30 to 40 minute ride out to the dive site in an inflatable, to sit around on site whilst divers are down and then have the same journey back in the wind and rain. On the return journey you may start off cold from your deep dive. You will be wet and exposed to the elements. If a cold wind is blowing and you are in a wet suit then it can be really uncomfortable. Even in a dry suit you will still feel the wind chill. You would be well advised to launch your boat at Houghton Bay, a natural harbour with a small slip and about the closest point to the German wrecks. It is only about ten minutes drive from Stromness, half-an-hour from Kirkwall and 40 minutes from Burray.

The *König* (IWM)

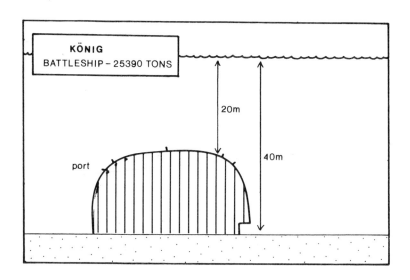

The Individual Wrecks of the High Seas Fleet

The *König*
(Battleship)

The *König* was one of the 11 battleships in the interned German High Seas Fleet. Of them three remain on the bottom today. The other two are the *Kronprinz Wilhelm* and *Markgraf*. The *König* was built by Kaiserliches Werft at the well known naval base of Wilhelmshaven which is situated on West Germany's small piece of coastline fronting the North Sea. She was launched on 1 March 1913 and officially completed on 10 August 1914. She had a displacement of 25,388 tons according to some sources and 25,800 tons according to others. She measured 575 feet in length with a beam of 97 feet and a draught of over 30 feet. Powered by three coal/oil-fired turbines, her three great propellers could drive the *König* to speeds of 23 knots.

She was heavily clad in 13.8-inch main-belt armour-plating. Another four inches of armour plating covered her decks. She boasted ten 12-inch guns in five twin turrets, all situated on the centre-line of the vessel, and each with a range of about 15,000 yards. These massive gun-turrets had 11.8-inch-thick protective armour plating. To supplement this firepower were 14 5.9-inch guns, six 3.45-inch guns and four 3.45-inch anti-aircraft guns. She also had five 19.7-inch submerged torpedo tubes, one in the bow and four in the beam. Her armoury was indeed awesome and keeping this vessel in fighting readiness required a complement of 1,136 officers and men.

The *König* had been the flagship of the Third Battleship Squadron (of three) that had formed the High Seas Fleet at the famous Battle of Jutland that took place in the North Sea in 1916 (christened by the Germans as the Battle of Skagerrak). This was the first major naval encounter between the British Grand Fleet and the German High Seas Fleet. The two fleets had been steaming in close proximity to one another, completely unaware of the other's presence. They were about 20 miles apart when a neutral Danish steamer steamed unwittingly in-between them and was spotted simultaneously by both sides, although the respective fleets could still not see one another. Light cruisers were sent out by both sides to investigate and as they closed on the steamer they each caught sight of the other's assembled fleets. Battle commenced at about 2.20 p.m. and raged throughout the afternoon as the two lines of battleships, each about eight miles long, wheeled and tried to out-manoeuvre each other. The *König*, *Markgraf* and the battlecruisers *Lützow* and *Derrflinger* took ten direct hits from 40 salvoes fired by the British battle group in one skirmish. The British cunningly set a trap and lured the German battle column towards them. Admiral Sir John Jellicoe in command of the British battle group then managed to accomplish the classic naval manoeuvre of 'crossing the T'. In this manoeuvre the whole British battle line managed to cross directly in the path of the German battle line. The result of this was that all the British ships could fire broadsides at the German line but only the lead German vessel could return fire. The German vanguard was faced with a complete line of British dreadnoughts belching fire at them. The British line stretched along the horizon to the north-east and north-west for as far as the Germans could see. Salvo followed salvo and a hail of fire rained down on the German vanguard. The *König*, the lead dreadnought of the vanguard, was badly hit many times and soon took on a $4\frac{1}{2}°$ list.

Skirmishing between the fleets continued after darkness had fallen and the last shots were fired at about 3.20 a.m. The battle had lasted for 11 hours during which the German High Seas Fleet had lost one pre-dreadnought battleship and one battle-cruiser, with 2,551 German sailors killed and 507 wounded.

The British Grand Fleet came off numerically worse with the loss of three battle-cruisers, three cruisers, one light cruiser and seven destroyers. A total of 6,097 British servicemen were killed in action, 510 were wounded and 177 British servicemen were taken prisoner by the Germans.

The statistics do not take account of the much higher ratio of damaged ships on the German side. The British retained undisputed mastery of the seas and the German High Seas Fleet was deterred from any further fleet action against the British as a result. The *König* continued to serve in the Fleet and was involved in the conquest of the Baltic Islands in the autumn of 1917. She sank at 2 p.m. on the day the Fleet was scuttled, 21 June 1919.

Today the *König* lies in about 40 metres of water east of Cava at Lat. 58° 53.13′ N and Long. 03° 09.07′ W. When she was scuttled the thousands of gallons of sea-water that poured into her altered her buoyancy and she became unstable. The colossal weight of her superstructure with its five main gun turrets weighing 600 tons each would have borne down to one side and the result was inevitable. Although, with her buoyancy intact she was very stable, she had now become top heavy and so she capsized and went down towards the sea-bed upside-down. The masts, guns and superstructure would have struck the sea-bed first and been driven into it by her 25,388 tons following down on top. As a result she now lies upside-down with her starboard side maindeck only a few feet above the bottom. Her superstructure is deeply embedded in the fine silty sea-bed with much of it being below the level of the sea-bed.

The least depth over her hull is about 20 metres. The whale-back of her upturned hull shelves off towards the bow and stern and the extent of the drop down to her hull really depends on where your skipper drops his shot-line. It is always exciting to drop into the water and start your descent with the shot-line stretching down into infinity. The descent before the hull comes into view seems to go on forever but then the blurred image of the hull seems to form before your eyes.

The *König* has been extensively salvaged over the years and much has been removed from her. The hull has been blown open as a result of the various efforts over more recent years to get at the valuable non-ferrous metal of the engine rooms and also to remove radiation-free steel for use in sensitive medical instruments. Nundy (Marine Metals) Ltd blasted open the hull in the vicinity of the engine and boiler rooms, the magazines and torpedo rooms, to let divers get access. Vast sections of plate appear to have been ripped off leaving a framework with huge gaping holes which give an insight into the innards of this mighty wreck. From above the bow torpedo tube, aft to the centre propeller shaft housing, the skin of the hull has been peeled off revealing the inner workings of the *König*. There is much indistinguishable wreckage littering the sea-bed around her—torn pipes, plates and spars. The blasting by the salvagers has left many torn and ragged edges to snag and tear at your dry suit. Like all the wrecks in Scapa Flow the structure is covered in a fine layer of silt which is easily stirred up into clouds. The holes and recesses in her structure appear black and foreboding, ready to trap the unwary.

The wreck of the *König* is colossal and will take several dives really to appreciate it. Do not be put off by her condition for she is an interesting dive.

Like most of the wrecks in Scapa Flow the *König* has become an artificial reef on the otherwise flattish silty bottom of the Flow and is now a home for a myriad of sea life from conger eels and wrasse to dead men's fingers and anemones which festoon entire sections of her. Large cod and saith will drift past you in the distance, perhaps inquisitive of the divers, visitors in their realm.

The *Kronprinz Wilhelm* with the *Markgraf* and *König* in the background

The *Kronprinz Wilhelm*
(Battleship)

Originally known simply as the *Kronprinz* she was built by Germaniawerft in Kiel. Launched on 21 February 1914 she was officially completed on 8 November 1914. The *Kronprinz* and her sister ships *König* and *Markgraf* were some of the largest dreadnoughts that the world had ever seen. So big were they that the Kiel Canal had to be specially widened to let them through after their completion. Her name was changed to the *Kronprinz Wilhelm* on 27 January 1918.

She had the same awesome specifications as her sister-ship the *König*, 575 feet long with a beam of 97 feet and a draught of over 30 feet. She displaced either 25,388 tons or 25,800 tons, according to differing reports. Her main armour belt was 13.8 inches thick and her deck had a 3.9-inch layer of armour plating on it. The gun-turrets and control tower had 11.8-inch protective armour plating. She bristled with fire power from her ten 12-inch main guns set in five twin turrets, to her 14 5.9-inch guns and her 3.45-inch anti-aircraft guns. Like the *König* she too had five submerged torpedo tubes, one to the bow and four in the beam.

Her 46,000 horsepower turbines drove three huge propellers that made the *Kronprinz* the fastest in her class with a top speed of about 21.3 knots. She needed a crew of 1,136 men to man her. She too formed part of the Third Battleship Squadron of the High Seas Fleet that took on the British at the Battle of Jutland, being the fourth in line of seven battleships. Although her sister-ships *König* and *Markgraf* were badly damaged in the thick of the battle, the *Kronprinz* came through unscathed and kept up a murderous hail of fire on the British battleships.

Apart from this crucial battle, the *Kronprinz* saw action on only one other occasion which she almost did not survive. At 10.30 p.m. on 4 November 1916 Admiral Hipper led the *Kronprinz* together with the *König*, *Markgraf* and *Grosser Kurfürst* out from the shelter of their base to support a squadron of destroyers which were going to the rescue of a U-boat which had run aground off the Danish coast. The scale of the operation was unusual and resulted from the presence of one man marooned in the U-boat. He was the U-boat commander Kapitanleutnant Walther Schwieger who had been responsible for one of the Great War's most infamous events, the torpedoing of the *Lusitania* with the loss of 1,198 men, women and children. The destroyers tried to tow *U-20* off but she was so well entrenched in the sand that their hawsers snapped. All other efforts to get her off failed, so the following morning her crew were taken off and she was blown up where she lay and at about 11 a.m. the battle group turned to head for home. At about 11.20 a.m. the group was spotted by the British submarine *J 1*, commanded by Commander Noel Laurence. At 12.08 p.m. he fired his first torpedo and successfully struck the *Grosser Kurfürst*. He fired a second time and again was deadly accurate. The torpedo hit the *Kronprinz*, blasting a gaping hole in her side. Both stricken battleships flooded with

The *Kronprinz Wilhelm*
(IWM)

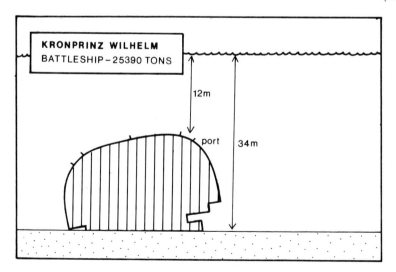

KRONPRINZ WILHELM
BATTLESHIP – 25390 TONS

12m

port

34m

tons of water and it was only their watertight compartments that prevented them from sinking and enabled them to limp back to the safe haven of their base. Both were out of action for several months as a result of Commander Laurence's daring piece of seamanship. In a fitting reward for his actions and for surviving two hours of depth-charging by the German destroyers he was awarded a bar to his DSO.

The *Kronprinz* spent most of the rest of the war at her moorings and by October 1918 the British blockade was strangling Germany and it had become clear that she was losing the war. She would be forced to try and negotiate a peaceful end to the war but a last-ditch battle was planned to try and inflict heavy losses on the British. The plan was for German destroyers to raid shipping off the coast of Flanders and the Thames Estuary while the main German battle fleet gathered at the Schillig Roadstead anchorage. It was hoped that the destroyer action would attract the British Grand Fleet and lure it towards Terschelling, a Dutch island some 70 miles from the Ems River estuary. In this killing, ground mines had already been sown and 25 U-boats lurked at the ready. Once they had inflicted damage on the British Grand Fleet the massive fire power of the German High Seas Fleet would be turned on to their unsuspecting and weakened foe.

The plan however was leaked and swept around the German sailors in the Fleet like wildfire, getting more and more exaggerated as it went. Soon there were rumours that the High Seas Fleet had accepted a British challenge for a fight to the death; that the 69-year-old Admiral Von Tirpitz had come out of retirement to take charge of the Fleet to lead it to its *Götterdämmerung* and even that the Kaiser himself would sail with the Fleet. The morale of the crews was very poor and they all realised that the war was lost. They were unwilling to risk their lives on a glorified but meaningless show of force. The crews of the *Kronprinz*, *König* and *Markgraf* refused to obey their orders to leave harbour. The mutiny spread and the plan was postponed as time after time the men refused to obey their orders to put to sea. In frustration, on 31 October, the German Command had the *U-135* lay off the *Thüringen* and threaten it with a salvo from its torpedo tubes. Two loyal destroyers tied up beside the *Thüringen* and 200 marines were put aboard. The mutineers fled to the forecastle and stood firm there. Other mutineers on the *Helgoland* trained its guns on the *U-135* and the destroyers. As the crisis escalated the mutineers on the *Helgoland* found to their astonishment the guns of the *Thüringen* now in the hands of loyal troops being trained on them. The stand-off lasted for some time until the mutineers gave way and some 500 men from the *Thüringen* and *Helgoland* were arrested.

The Third Squadron with the *Kronprinz*, *König* and *Markgraf* were sent to Kiel as the Fleet was dispersed. There mutiny flared again and this time as the rebellion grew it won the support of the townspeople. On 4 November the mutineers won control of Kiel. The rebellion spread from town to town with communist red flags appearing everywhere. On 9 November the Kaiser abdicated and gave way to a communist régime. At 5 a.m. on Monday 11 November 1918 the Armistice bringing the hostilities to an end was signed. For such great fighting ships as these dreadnoughts, this was an inglorious end to their war service. By the time she was scuttled in June 1919, the *Kronprinz* was a poor shadow of her former self. She had a skeleton crew of only about 200 men, and her guns had been disarmed before she had set off from Germany for internment in Scapa Flow, so she was no longer an effective fighting force. She finally slipped beneath the waves to her present resting place at 1.15 p.m. on the day of the scuttling.

Today the *Kronprinz Wilhelm* lies capsized in about 34 metres of water at Lat. 58° 53 39.0′ N. and Long. 03° 09 46.0′ W. She lies on her starboard maindeck with much of her superstructure embedded in the silty bottom. The drop down from the surface to the highest point of her upturned whale-back hull is about 12 to 15 metres. She is not such a deep dive as the *König* or *Markgraf* but is a thoroughly exciting dive nevertheless. She is also in better condition than the *König* and *Markgraf*. She has a flattish hull with four noticeable protruding bilge-keels. The hull slopes off quite severely at the bow and stern. There is a fair amount of damage to her hull in the vicinity of the engine rooms, boiler rooms, and torpedo rooms, the result of blasting by salvagers allowing divers to get access to the valuable non-ferrous metals in these areas. In particular there is a large hole about 15 metres across blasted in her port side about two thirds of the way back towards her stern which is fringed by torn plating. The structural stringers or ribs are clearly visible inside. At the bow and stern her plating has been torn open leaving ominous, black, seemingly bottomless, holes. Her hull is otherwise intact bar some plating being buckled and bent in places.

When you first arrive on the hull of the *Kronprinz* after your descent from the surface you seem to land on the sea-bed as the hull has a covering of silt, and sponges and anemones abound in profusion. The regular lines of rivets sticking up and the solid unyielding feel to the silt reveal the fact that you are actually on the surface of a man-made platform. Plenty of natural light filters down to her here. Finning over the side of the hull the vessel drops away sharply and you become aware that in the shadow of the hull below you it is black and gloomy. As you drop down the port side of the hull your eyes become used to the gloom as you adjust your buoyancy to regulate your descent. At about 30 metres the inverted bulwark rail of the ship comes into view, marking the end of the hull. From here the deck runs in below the vessel towards the superstructure embedded in the silt. If you thought dropping over the side of the hull was black then this takes that concept even further! Without a torch it is difficult to make out any features under the deck and in any event their being upside-down complicates the position further. The sea-bed at 35 metres is easily visible beneath you and between the sea-bed and the bulwark rail is a yawning black chasm running right the way along the hull on the port side. It will take several dives on this wreck to know exactly where you are on her and to identify the parts of the superstructure that are underneath the hull but not embedded in the silt. The after superimposed 12-inch gun-turret can be made out, its top buried in the sea-bed and the twin gun barrels half-covered by silt. Further aft can be found the aftmost 12-inch gun-turret with both its barrels clear of the sea-bed, their ends jammed into the teak deck-planking above.

Swimming along the bulwark rail you will see rows of portholes, some still in place, countersunk with brass screws. The *Kronprinz* had many secondary side gun-turrets along her bulwark rail and these were actually part of the structure of the hull. Several of these turrets can be seen as you swim along the bulwark rail.

Just aft of the bridge the four-foot wide mainmast can be seen lying on the sea-bed at 90° to the hull. It is practically intact and the cross rigging lies nearby. Finning along the mast away from the hull you will come across the spotting top or crow's nest. The sea-bed along both sides of the great hull is littered with wreckage and rigging.

All in all the *Kronprinz* makes an exciting dive for many reasons. The sea life is good, the immensity of her size will dwarf anyone diving her and for wreck ferrets there is so much to see and explore. She should not be missed. My log-book entry for my first-ever dive on her many years ago still rings true for me today. 'Raining heavily with slightly

The *Markgraf* (IWM)

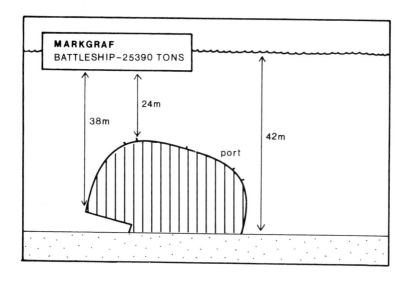

choppy seas. First-ever dive on a battleship—really immense—difficult to grasp the scale of it. Lots of dark holes to explore. We only scratched the surface of it. You would need a dozen dives on it really to get to know it.'

The *Markgraf*
(Battleship)

The battleship *Markgraf* was built in Germany by A. G. Weser at Bremen to the same specifications as the *König* and *Kronprinz Wilhelm*. She was launched on 4 June 1913 and officially completed on 1 October 1914. She formed part of the Third Battleship Squadron and took part in the conquest of the Baltic Islands in 1917. Displacing 25,388 tons, she was a formidable foe to face. In effect she was a floating fighting platform and with her arsenal of armaments could train a murderous hail of fire on the enemy. She was 575 feet long with a beam of 97 feet and a draught of 30 feet. Her three coal/oil turbines drove three huge propellers which could force the colossal weight of the *Markgraf* through the water at speeds of up to 21 knots. She boasted ten 12-inch guns set in five twin turrets, 14 5.9-inch guns, six 3.45-inch guns and four 3.45-inch anti-aircraft guns. To complement that firepower she had five 19.7-inch submerged torpedo tubes constantly ready for action, one at the bow and four to her beam. To keep this warship functioning as an effective fighting force required a crew of some 1,136 officers and men.

The *Markgraf* along with the *König*, *Kronprinz Wilhelm* and the other battleships of the Third Battleship Squadron traditionally formed the vanguard of the German battle line and so took part in some of the heaviest fighting in the Battle of Jutland. She was hit many times as Admiral Jellicoe succeeded in manoeuvring his eight-mile-long battle formation into position to carry out the classic naval manoeuvre of 'crossing the T'. The entire British battle line crossed in front of the German vanguard and was able to fire broadside after broadside at the German vanguard with only the lead warships of the German line able to return fire.

It was the *Markgraf* that was boarded on 21 June 1919 by a Royal Marine boarding party as she began to settle into the water after the scuttling had started. The Royal Marines had their orders to stop the warship sinking and once aboard confronted the *Markgraf*'s captain, Lt-Cdr Walther Schumann who was busy helping to complete the final operations to ensure that she sank. He eventually emerged from below deck waving a white flag but refused to obey orders from the Marines to have his own men go below and shut off the flood valves or indeed to allow the Marines to go below and do just that. A scuffle broke out in which Schumann was shot through the head by a Royal Marine. His fleet engineer Faustmann managed to stay below and complete the work and the *Markgraf* went to the bottom at about 4.45 p.m. Lt-Cdr Schumann's grave can be seen at the Royal Naval Cemetery at Lyness on the island of Hoy, along with the graves of the other German sailors who died that day and many British seamen from both wars.

Today the *Markgraf* lies upturned, resting on her port side maindeck at Lat. 58° 53 31.0′ N and Long. 3° 09 55.0′ W and like nearly all of the German Fleet faces WNW. The depth to the sea-bed is about 45 metres and the least depth over her is about 24 metres. Some time spent placing the shot on the shallowest part of the upturned hull will pay dividends. The hull shelves off quite steeply to the stern and bow, where there is a drop of about 33 metres until you hit the hull. This will considerably lessen your bottom time and there is much to see at the midships shallowest region. It is important on this wreck that you do not haul yourself down the shot-line. The practice with the local skippers is to use quite a light weight as a shot as it makes it easier to get up. The hull of the *Markgraf* is quite smooth with no real features to snag the shot. Careless pulling of the shot can wrench it right off the hull and it will then drop to the sea-bed at 45 metres. Instead of a good wreck dive you will find yourself doing a bounce dive on the silty sea-bed beside the *Markgraf*! As you descend towards the hull the shot-line disappears beneath you into the darkness below. After what seems like an eternity the flat silty sea-bed seems to appear beneath you and it is only when you land on the unyielding bottom that it becomes apparent that this is not the sea-bed but is in fact the massive silt-covered hull of the *Markgraf*. Looking carefully you can make out the regular rows of rivets on the plating and a large anchor chain runs from the bow, along the top of the hull, nearly all the way to the stern, further proof that this is not a natural phenom-enon that you are resting on. As far as the eye can see all around, it is seemingly flat but as you get orientated you become aware that although from above the hull appeared to be flat, it in fact shelves off gradually towards the port side. Swimming towards the drop over the side of the hull, one of the bilge keels appears, a strip of steel about nine inches high running along practically the entire length of the hull and designed to give the otherwise flattish hull a cutting edge for manoeuvring through the water. Past this and the hull disappears almost in a sheer drop beneath you down to the sea-bed at 45 metres.

It is a feature of Scapa Flow wreck-diving that the wrecks are so large that they cast a considerable shadow to the dark side. As you peer over the side of the *Markgraf's* hull the sea-bed is still over 20 metres below you and cannot be seen. Consequently the side of the hull just disappears into the darkness. Once you have dropped over the side of the hull the feeling is similar to wall diving. There are a lot of holes and features at every level of the hull and by adjusting your buoyancy it is possible to hang motionless beside the hull or descend to see what lies below out of eyeshot. As you descend down the port side at about 30 metres down, the heavy armour plating has been peeled off in a row for a considerable distance along the hull from near the bow to midships, its mountings rotted. The plating has dropped down in sheets and now juts out at right angles to the sheer face of the hull, making a platform on which you can rest. Peering in through the yawning gaps left by this reveals a gap of about three metres and then the ribbed inner bulkheads. At about 35 metres there is another similar area where the plating has been peeled outwards to lie at right angles to the hull.

The hull is generally in good condition and is mainly whole. At the bow a large hole has been blasted by salvagers and the strong thick plating of her hull has been peeled back like cardboard. At the very tip the bow plunges off dramatically into the darkness below. About two-thirds of the way back towards the stern, in the vicinity of the engine room, a huge hole about 15 metres by 15 metres has been blasted by salvagers and as you swim over it you can just see the other side at the limit of your vision. Beneath you is a black yawning chasm dropping down through a number of decks, holding many fascinating secrets and revealing something of the innards of the hull.

The hull on the port side actually rests on the sea-bed, so on this side you can get no glimpse of the superstructure of the vessel. On the starboard side of the hull as you descend, the hull stops abruptly at the bulwark rail in about 38 metres of water. From here down to the sea-bed at 45 metres is a seven-metre-high chasm. The teak-planked deck runs off sharply under the hull, creating a black, eerie cave under the

The *Brummer* (IWM)

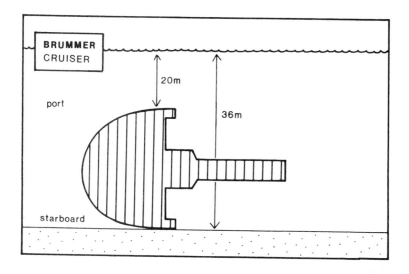

overhanging deck. To venture under here, a torch is essential. The sheer drop from the bulwark rail to the sea-bed reveals part of the superstructure of the battleship. Being upside down it is difficult to recognise any features in the little time you have at this depth. The midship's 12-inch gun-turret can be found half-buried in the shale with the starboard crane stanchion just aft of it.

The *Markgraf* is a very scenic dive with many sponges and anemones covering parts of it. The hull is home to a wide variety of crustacean life and occasionally large cod will drift past in the distance. It is an exhilarating wreck to dive and on a diving trip to Scapa Flow should positively not be missed.

The *Brummer*
(Light cruiser, Bremse class)

The *Brummer* was a 'Kleiner Kruizer' or fast mine-laying cruiser built at Stettin by A. G. Vulcan. Launched on 11 December 1915 she was completed in 1916. She displaced 4,308 tons and, driven by her two sets of turbines and twin propellers, she could achieve speeds of up to 28 knots. She therefore lived up to her name, *Brummer*, which means 'wasp' in German. She measured 462 feet in length with a beam of 44 feet and a draught of 20 feet. She was built for speed and so to keep her weight down she was obviously far less well protected than the battleships with their 13.8-inch armour plating. The *Brummer* had only 1.6-inch main belt armour plating. Her all important control tower had 3.9-inch armour plating and the armoured deck had 0.6-inch plating. She was armed with four 5.9-inch guns in single mountings (two forward and two to the stern), and two 3.4-inch anti-aircraft guns between the after funnels and mainmast. She was one of eight light cruisers that scuttled with the Fleet in 1919 and yet only one, the *Bremse*, was ever salvaged. Three were beached and the remaining four—*Dresden*, *Köln*, *Karlsruhe* and the *Brummer*—still lie on the bottom of Scapa Flow.

The *Brummer* was heavily involved during her war years in the disruption of trade and naval convoys between Great Britain and Norway, working hand in hand often with the *Bremse*. She had a crew of 309 officers and men.

Today the *Brummer* rests in 36 metres of water on the starboard side of her hull, heading WNW. She is therefore completely accessible and is generally in good condition despite damage in a few places where salvagers have carried out blasting. Around the port bow and accessible port side of her hull the plating is torn and buckled. The holes in her side look black and ominous. The upward-facing port side of the hull is lined with rows of portholes.

The least depth over her is about 20 metres to her upward-facing port side. The large 5.9-inch bow deck-gun is still in good condition, set in its single turret on the centre line of the vessel at about 30 metres down. Her two masts are broken and now rest on the sea-bed. They still have their antennae, lamps and range-finders in place. Her propellers have been removed at some time in the past. Her forward anchor chains which would have been run out when she was moored in the Flow before the scuttling, run out from the chain lockers below decks to the circular steam capstans. From there they lead out through circular apertures in the deck, the hull hawse pipes, to where they once would have held anchors in place. The port anchor chain is slack and loops downwards dramatically before rising up and disappearing through the hull hawse pipe to the top port side of the wreck. Above and below the steam capstans, twin mooring bollards are located. Immediately behind the steam capstans is a large opening and peering into it and looking downwards you can see brighter green far below, contrasting with the black of the interior of the wreck and indicating that it is open below.

Immediately behind the bow gun-turret, the 3.9-inch armoured control tower, with its thin viewing slits ringed round it, juts out at right angles to the wood-lined and now vertical deck. From the greater safety of this protected area the captain and officers would have directed operations when the *Brummer* was in battle. Behind the control tower the superstructure of the bridge, mainmast and cross-rigging remains in place although the bridge has partially collapsed. The *Brummer* although substantially intact has had extensive blasting carried out by salvagers in the vicinity of her engine room and boiler rooms, opening her up. It is possible to swim into these wide-open areas and get a feel of the inner size of the vessel. Her two stern 5.9-inch gun-turrets remain in position.

The wreck of the *Brummer* lies not far from the rocky islet in the middle of the Flow, known as the Barrel of Butter. A colony of seals has made this their home and occasionally on your slow ascent from the wrecks seals will dart around you. Generally they are inquisitive but wary of coming too close to these strange visitors to their underwater realm. Occasionally

The wreck of the
Brummer

some of the bolder will come in quite close perhaps taking a playful nibble at your fins.

The *Köln*
(Light cruiser, Dresden II class)

Built in Hamburg by Blohm & Voss, the *Köln* was launched on 5 October 1916 and completed in 1918. She displaced 5,531 tons and measured 510 feet in length with a beam of 47 feet and a draught of 21 feet. She was powered by two sets of coal/oil-fired turbines and twin propellers. She could achieve speeds of more than 29 knots, and was protected by 2.4-inch main belt and deck armour. The control tower, the nerve centre of the vessel, was protected by thicker 3.9-inch armour. She was heavily armed with eight 5.9-inch guns in single mountings, two at the bow, one either side of the bridge and also the mainmast, two on the centre line at the stern and three 3.4-inch anti-aircraft guns. She had four 23.6-inch torpedo tubes mounted on her deck, one either side of the foremast and also just aft of the aftermast funnel, and carried

The *Köln* (IWM)

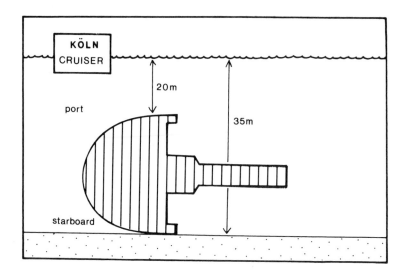

about 200 mines. She was therefore considerably bigger and more heavily armed than the *Brummer*. Correspondingly, she carried a larger crew of 559 officers and men. She sank at 1.50 p.m. on 21 June 1919.

Today the *Köln* lies in 35 metres of water, resting on her starboard side and heading WNW. The least depth over her upward-facing port side is about 20 metres and she is in such good condition that she is regarded as one of the finest dives in the Flow and a wreck that is visited time and time again by divers. She is almost completely intact, barring her propellers and anchors which were salvaged some time ago and a large hole blasted in her near the stern. She is an impressive vessel and still has lots of brass fittings clearly visible on her deck. Rows of portholes line the uppermost port side of her hull. There are many openings and doorways to her interior. Beware, however, as one of my buddy divers, once, without warning, swam a short way down one of these passages from the deck. He later recounted that as he finned down the passageway the water ahead of him was crystal clear and that the passageway soon opened out into a much larger area. He stopped after a short distance and turned round to come out only to be met by a solid wall of silt stirred up by his fin strokes coming down the corridor towards him. The cloud of silt swept over him and immediately his visibility was reduced to nil. He quickly became disorientated and unable to remember the way out. The position was confused even further by everything being on its side. The last thing I saw of him was his fins disappearing into a cloud of silt. I swam to the entrance of the passageway and shone my torch down the corridor without actually going inside and into the silt. When the silt started to settle he was able to see the faint beam of my torch in the distance and make his way out. Fortunately he had not gone in too far. He swam back down the passage-way towards my torch beam and I only saw him when he appeared out of the cloud of silt about six inches from my face.

The bow of the *Köln* is sleek and narrow and is festooned with sponges and anemones. The two forward anchor chains rise from chain lockers and run out to circular steam capstans. From here they run through their hawse pipes in the deck to the side of the vessel where the anchors would once have been held. From here one chain has run out and now drops straight down to the sea-bed nine metres below where it is run out for some distance. Twin mooring bollards are set at the side of the hull nearby.

The *Köln* originally had two 5.9-inch guns at the bow but these would appear to have been successfully salvaged, as located just behind the two capstans are the remnants of their wracking systems. Immediately aft of this sits the almost oval armoured control tower with its thin viewing slits on two levels ringing completely around it. I must confess that when I first dived the *Köln* I could not reconcile this feature with any of the photographs of her that are available. My immediate reaction was that she had been altered after the photographs were taken or that the vessel in the photographs available was not the *Köln*. The photographs of the *Köln* that are available show no such feature but reveal a bridge area with what appears to be a walkway protected with steel sheeting around it. What I now think has happened is that the lighter and thinner protective steel sheeting of the walkway around the bridge or control tower has rusted off, or been torn by salvagers, leaving only the far stronger armour of the oval control tower in place. On top of the second level of the control tower sits a winged instrument, the central gun-control range-finder.

Immediately aft of the control tower the superstructure and mainmast with its cross-rigging remains intact, bar a few twisted and burst open plates. Still in place on the foremast can be seen the steel searchlight platforms. Set in the wood-lined deck immediately aft of the foremast is an open companionway hatch which once would have led into the innards of the vessel but is now filled in with silt. It still has its steps with their brass treads in place. There is no trace of the three funnels in their original positions but the sea-bed beneath this area is littered with debris. On the topmost port side of the hull, empty lifeboat davits hang outwards, their lifeboats having been lowered as the vessel was scuttled.

Just aft of the area where the funnels once stood at the side of the mainmast, stands a 5.9-inch gun-turret, the barrel pointing upwards at an angle towards the distant surface. The raised decking on which this gun-turret stood has corroded away revealing the cylindrical housing for the turret's turning mechanism which runs horizontally towards the main deck.

The mainmast and its large circular viewing platform are set at an angle to the main wreck and mark the start of the largest blasted hole in this wreck, in the engine room area. The hull stops abruptly where the plating has been torn open and there are many sharp edges. The hole is about 12 metres square and the blurred shape of the hull re-forms at the limit of your vision. Just beyond this hole and near the stern the 5.9-inch

The wreck of the Köln

gun turret on the raised stern bulkhead appears with its barrel and breech in good condition and encrusted with sea life. A now horizontal doorway is situated in this bulkhead in what was the officers' accommodation. Its heavy hinged door lies open on the bulkhead itself. Rows of portholes give glimpses into the *Köln*'s cavernous interior. Just as the extended gun barrel comes to an end the bulkhead itself ends and on the main deck below another 5.9-inch gun-turret, complete with barrel and breech, is situated. Underneath its barrel the stern anchor capstan is located and the rounded stern of the vessel looms into sight. Mooring bollards and cleets are dotted around the edge of the main deck here.

The *Dresden*
(Light cruiser, Dresden II class)

Built at Kiel by Howaldtswerke, the *Dresden* was launched on 25 April 1917 and completed in 1918 when she went into service with the Fleet. She was of the same Dresden II class as

The *Dresden* (IWM)

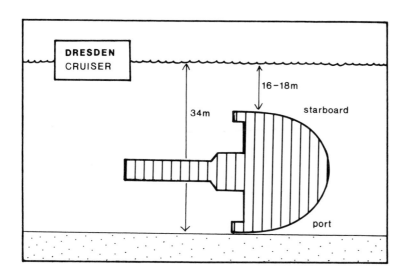

the *Köln*. She displaced 5,531 tons and powered by her two sets of coal/oil fired turbines, her twin propellers could achieve speeds of up to 28 knots.

Protected by 2.4-inch armour plating around her main belt, her deck had a similar 2.4-inch protective layer of armour. Her control tower was more heavily armoured with 3.9-inch thick armour. The *Dresden* boasted eight 5.9-inch guns in single turrets, two at the bow, one either side of the bridge and also the mainmast, and two on the centre line at the stern. She also had three 3.4-inch anti-aircraft guns. She carried four deck-mounted 23.6-inch torpedo tubes, one either side of the foremast and also just aft of the aftermost funnel. With her speed and manoeuvrability she was ideal as a mine layer to evade enemy action and yet heavily enough armed to ward off most foes. As a result the *Dresden* would normally carry about 200 mines and carried a crew of 559 officers and men.

She was normally moored during internment near the rocky outcrop in the centre of the Flow known as the Barrel of Butter. Once the British discovered that the Fleet was scuttling, the drifter *Clonsin* took the *Dresden* in tow even though she was so low in the water that her decks were awash. The progress of the *Clonsin* was made painfully slow by the dead weight of the *Dresden* which was filling rapidly with water. She was so low that she had to be dragged through the water rather than slicing through it as normal. The *Clonsin* made for the island of Cava which was less than a mile away. On the way the *Dresden* continued to flood and when she was about half way between the Barrel of Butter and Cava, she lurched down by the head and then capsized and sank so quickly that there was no time to cast off the towing cable. She sank at 11.30 a.m. on 21 June 1919.

Today the *Dresden* lies in 34 metres of water resting on her port side and makes as good a dive as the *Köln*. You can get orientated easily and she is largely intact with many of her original features still in place. The least depth over her is about 16 to 18 metres. Being relatively shallow she has a rich covering of marine growth and entire sections of her, such as the bow, are completely covered in sponges and anemones. At the bow the anchor chains are run out, their huge links still leading from the chain lockers to the two circular anchor capstans. From here the port anchor chain drops straight down for 10 metres to the sea-bed where it runs out along the sea-bed for some way. The starboard anchor chain leads out from the capstan and disappears through the hawse pipe in

the deck. The rakish lines of the bow itself present a sleek profile designed for slicing through the water. Remnants of the original deck-hand rail still ring around the bow itself and the flat carpet of sea growth is only interrupted by the sudden appearance of twin bow mooring bollards at the very edge of the main deck. The *Dresden* originally had two 5.9-inch gun-turrets just forward of her bridge at the bow. Like the *Köln* these would appear to have been salvaged success-fully.

The wreck of the *Dresden*

The bridge of the *Dresden* is fairly intact and the armoured control tower with its viewing slits situated in amongst the superstructure of the bridge reminds divers that this was an armoured warship. Ringing round the control tower about three metres off the main deck is the open viewing platform and a similar distance above is a second but smaller semi-circular observation platform. The foremast is still intact and resting on the sea-bed. It runs out at the back of the bridge from the main deck and still has its original cross-rigging in place and two circular searchlight platforms. Cables run from various points of the mast to the bridge and deck. At the base of the bridge on the starboard side of the hull a 5.9-inch gun-turret can be found with its barrel facing forward and resting on the superstructure of the bridge beneath it. Steel ladder rungs run up the side of the bridge superstructure just beside it to give access to the viewing platform above. Two rows of port holes run along the complete length of the hull. Aft of the bridge were originally three funnels. In this area there is a cavernous black hole, a result of salvaging the condensers and other non-ferrous metal. Rows of square windows, the glass gone, line the officer's accommodation towards the stern. Open doorways, now horizontal, give access for the experienced diver. The stern is relatively intact with both gun-turrets still in place. The stern anchor still sits in its hawse.

The *Karlsruhe*
(Light cruiser, Konigsberg II class)

Built at Wilhelmshaven by Kaiserliches Werft, the *Karlsruhe* was launched on 31 January 1916. She took part in the campaign in the autumn of 1917 that resulted in the conquest of the Baltic Islands. She was slightly lighter than the *Köln* and *Dresden* displacing 5,354 tons. Driven by two coal/oil-fired turbines, her two propellers could push her to speeds of nearly 28 knots. She was protected by a 2.4-inch thick layer of armour plating on her main belt and on her deck. Her control tower had a 3.9-inch layer of protective armour plating.

She carried eight 5.9-inch guns in single turrets. Of these, two were set at the bow, two were set one at either side of the bridge facing forward, two faced astern at either side of the deck, just forward of the mainmast, and two were set astern on the centre line of the vessel. There were two 3.5-inch anti-aircraft guns and two 19.7-inch deck-mounted torpedo tubes. Like the *Köln* and *Dresden* she too carried about 200 mines. She had an operational crew complement of 475 officers and men.

The two *Dresden* II class destroyers *Köln* and *Dresden* had their heavily-armoured control towers incorporated into the superstructure of the bridge and this would have facilitated better communications with the crew and an ability for officers to get up to the higher observation platform quickly and of course to get off it quickly and into the safety of the control tower if the vessel came under fire. The *Brummer*

The *Karlsruhe* (IWM)

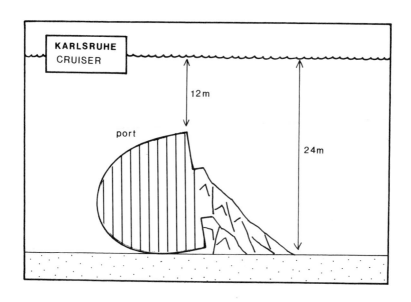

The wreck of the
Karlsruhe

and *Karlsruhe* had a markedly different arrangement. The control tower was set on the main deck some distance forward of the bridge superstructure. If a direct hit was scored on the bridge, by an enemy, the armoured control tower would be able to withstand the blast and so the ship would not be disabled. The *Karlsruhe* sank at 3.50 p.m. on 21 June 1919.

Today the *Karlsruhe* lies in about 26 metres of water off the northerly tip of Cava with its conspicuous white lighthouse. She rests on her starboard side and is a shallower dive than the *Dresden*, *Brummer* or *Köln*. She has a least depth over her of about 12 to 14 metres. There is a four-metre difference in depth between the bottom on the keel side and the deeper deck side, presumably as a result of scouring or a sloping bottom. Unlike the other light cruisers she is heavily damaged as a result of extensive blasting by salvagers. Only her stern section remains relatively intact. As a result of the blasting and the consequent collapse of the deck the two side-by-side bow gun-turrets are now staggered with one of them lying on the sea-bed and the fire-control tower and detached masts lying nearby. The starboard anchor chain lies run out on the sea-bed for some distance as it would have fallen as the vessel sank during the scuttling, with the anchor itself embedded in the silt at its end. The uppermost port side of her hull is now almost horizontal and the deck with its original wood planking still visible sits almost vertically, at right angles to the sea-bed. A pronounced bilge keel about a metre high juts out from the hull and runs for some distance along it.

Towards the stern a large hole has been blasted into the hull and inside there is a jumble of cogs and gearing mechanisms, signifying that this is probably the engine room. Near this area steam-driven circular capstans and mooring bollards are visible. One 5.9-inch gun and a smaller 2.4-inch gun can be found here. Amidships an even bigger hole has been blasted, removing about a quarter of the length of the hull. This area is a mass of tangled spars and wreckage with nothing really recognisable and the wreck completely loses its ship shape. Moving towards the bow the shape of the vessel reforms before your eyes with a mass of torn and twisted plates. The effects of the blasting have left a big cavern underneath the topside of the hull.

The wood-lined deck is at 90° to the sea-bed and nearly everything has been blown or torn off it. There are however a great number of open hatches and holes to peer into. The sea-bed is littered with torn plates, spars and the debris that the salvagers have left. Horse mussels, scallops and queenies abound everywhere. Don't be put off by the condition of this wreck. It is a very interesting dive.

The V 83
(Torpedo-boat destroyer, V 67–84 class)

The V 83 lies away from the other German wrecks on the east side of Rysa Little. She was built by A. G. Vulcan at Hamburg and entered service in the High Seas Fleet in 1916. She displaced 909 tons and was 269 feet long with a beam of 27 feet and a draught of 13 feet. She was powered by two oil-fired turbines driving two propellers. Being much lighter than the bigger cruisers she could easily outpace them and achieve speeds in excess of 36 knots. She was armed with three 3.4-inch guns and six 19.7-inch deck-mounted torpedo tubes. Being fast and manoeuvrable she was useful as a mine-layer and generally carried about 24 mines. She had a ship's complement of 87 officers and men and formed part of the Seventh Torpedo-boat Flotilla. In internment the torpedo-boats were moored by flotilla and were chained together in twos and threes at any one mooring buoy, with only one of the group occupied to economise on fuel. Of the 50 torpedo boats moored in the Flow, 32 sank and 18 were beached or were scuttled in water so shallow that they were not completely submerged. When Cox started his salvage operations he found that the destroyers were heaped in piles on top of each other on the sea-bed and it was this that led the 'experts' to conclude that they could never be lifted. Cox of course was to prove them wrong.

Cox was to use the salvaged *V 83* in his many attempts (see Chapter 2) to raise the colossal *Hindenburg* which had been scuttled not far away between the Islands of Hoy and Cava. Once the *Hindenburg* had been lifted the *V 83* was dumped in her present position.

Today the *V 83* is broken into two distinct sections. She sits on a shelving bottom so that her bows are in five to eight metres of water and her stern is in about 20 metres. She is broken in half amidships with her stern in reasonable condition. The bow points towards the shore and rests on its port side. Being so shallow, the bow is well covered with kelp but in amongst the kelp the rakish lines of the bow can be made out along with hatches and companionways.

The midships section is well broken up and is hardly recognisable as a result of extensive salvaging over the years. It is a jumble of twisted plates and wreckage. In the midst of this wreckage one of her 3.4-inch guns and its cogged wracking system lies with the barrel pointing upwards at an angle of about 45°. To her port side in this area lies one of her boilers. Along almost the entire port side on top of much of the wreckage lies the main flanged prop shaft. In this area from the bow to midships the remnants of the torpedo tubes can be picked out amidst the debris.

About 12 metres of the stern section remains intact. The hull is open in many places here with only the ribs of the vessel in place. The stern section sits on an even keel and at its very extremity rests on its rudder with the prop shafts for each of its twin screws visible at either side of it.

The *V 83* is close to Lyness by boat and is popular as a second dive because it is relatively shallow compared to the rest of the Fleet. She is quite a small wreck and is easily covered in one dive with time to spare at the end to potter about in amongst the wreckage.

There are two other of the torpedo-boats scuttled in Scapa Flow still remaining today, the S 36 on North House, Cava and the S 54 on the east side of Flotta. Of the S 36 only the bow section remains and lies in shallow water. The S 54 rests in 16 metres of water and has been well smashed up by the salvagers' blasting and storms. Neither of these wrecks is really worth visiting if your time at Scapa Flow is limited.

The gun-turrets of the *Bayern*

The 28,000 ton battleship *Bayern* was the latest state of the art in warship construction when she came into service in the High Seas Fleet. She had a formidable arsenal of weaponry at her disposal, not least her eight powerful 15-inch guns set in four twin turrets. In June 1933 Metal Industries Ltd attempted to salvage her but found that she, like the other battleships, had turned turtle as she sank because of the enormous weight of her fighting top bearing her over to one side as the water flooded into her. She therefore lay with the bottom of her hull facing upwards and much of her superstructure embedded in the sea-bed beneath. After 14 years on the sea-bed she was well settled into the mud and silt and was held firm by its inexorable grip. During the course of the salvage operations a compressed air hosepipe burst inside the hull of the vessel and the sunken hull of the vessel filled with compressed air. This made the hull buoyant and it strained to break free from the grip of the sea-bed. With a sudden upwards movement the *Bayern* tore free of the suction of the sea-bed and started rising quickly to the surface.

The sudden strain put on the vessel as it lay held by the mud of the sea-bed meant that something had to give. It is difficult to comprehend the titanic forces that were at work at this time. The shock of the upward force tore the gun-turrets off her and they fell to the sea-bed where they still lie to this day. Once on the surface, with the decrease in pressure, the surplus air could escape from the hull and the *Bayern* then became negatively buoyant and sank to the sea-bed once again. Eventually after three months' further painstaking work the *Bayern* was ready to make a controlled ascent to the surface. This time everything went according to plan. The *Bayern* lifted off the sea-bed and shot to the surface in about 30 seconds.

Diver examines porthole on the Kronprinz Wilhelm *at 30 metres*

The breech of the 5.9-inch stern gun on the Köln

Go *no further*

Festooned deck valve on the Brummer

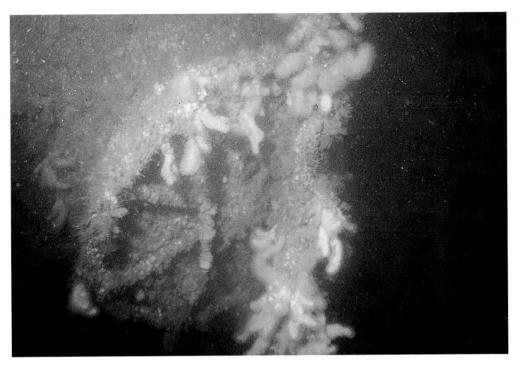

Forward anchor capstan on the Köln with festooned anchor chain plunging down from above

An open companionway hatch, aft of the bridge of the Köln, still has its steps in place

Torpedo framework on deck of the Brummer

Diver examines viewing slit on the bridge of the Köln *at 28 metres*

Inside the Gobernador Bories *at 16 metres*

Feeding friendly wrasse on the Gobernador Bories

The torn plating on the Roedean *is home for a rich variety of marine life*

Mooring bollard on the wreck of the Roedean

Diver descends over kelp forest near the bow of the V 83

The huge camshaft of the Empire Seaman

The wreck of the Inverlane *with (inset) view on board*

The striking wreck of the Pontos

The four turrets of the *Bayern* each weigh about 600 tons and they lie in about 35 metres of water not far from the *Kronprinz Wilhelm*. They lie upside down embedded in the silty sea-bed where they fell off the rising *Bayern*. The barrels of the guns themselves are buried in the silt and cannot be seen but the inner workings and mechanisms of the turrets themselves lie wide open for examination. The enormous cogged wracking system that turned each turret rises up at 90° from the centre of the turrets and ends in jagged and torn metal where it was torn from the deck of the battleship itself.

Diving the High Seas Fleet scrapyard

When the High Seas Fleet was scuttled on that fateful day, 21 June 1919, those of the heavier warships with large superstructures and heavy gun-turrets became unstable as they flooded with water. The battleships generally turned turtle as they went down and as examples of this the three battleships *Kronprinz Wilhelm*, *Markgraf* and *König* sit today on the sea-bed inverted with the bottom of their hulls facing upwards. The light destroyers, like the *Köln* and *Brummer* had no such fighting tops and generally they slipped under the water and sank in a more upright position.

The great salvage effort that followed spanned 25 years, from 1920 to 1945. By the time many of the vessels were lifted they had been on the bottom for a number of years and as a result much had fallen or rotted off them and dropped to lie on the sea-bed. When the great inverted battleships were lifted many movable bits and pieces were left on the sea-bed underneath where they had lain and the sites were forgotten about.

Over the last few years many of the sites have been rediscovered by dive-boat operators who have found the large depressions in the sea-bed that mark where they lie. The sites have been identified and now provide a fascinating experience for today's sports divers. The sea-bed is littered with all sorts of debris ranging from 50-feet-long tender vessels known as pinnaces, complete with original bronze propellers, to brass mast lamps and other smaller pieces. Understandably these sites have been nicknamed by the local skippers as the 'scrapyards'. The exact locations of these scrapyards are really only known to the local skippers and you will have to prevail on them if you want an opportunity to dive them.

Alternative Wreck Dives

UB-116

LOCATION: PAN HOPE

The *UB-116* was a German coastal submarine of the UB-III class which was sunk on 28 October 1918. She had the misfortune of being the last naval vessel sunk in the Scapa Flow area in the First World War. She had been sent to Scapa Flow, and to her doom, on a mission to penetrate the British naval defences in Hoxa Sound and sink any British warships and merchant vessels in the Flow at the time. German intelligence believed that Hoxa Sound, which is the main deep entrance to the Flow from the south, was not protected by boom-nets or a mine-field. The German intelligence was to be proved fatally flawed. As the *UB-116* tried to slip into the Flow through Hoxa Sound, the noise generated by her motors was picked up on sensitive British listening devices called hydrophones. Once an enemy had been heard entering the Flow all the British defences were put on full alert to locate the intruder. Just before midnight she was picked up again by a detector loop. These were cables laid throughout the Flow which could determine precisely when a vessel passed overhead. Once the intruder's position had been detected the British were able to set off a mine by remote control in the hope of destroying her.

When daylight came the following day it was found that oil and bubbles of air were rising from the location of the explosion. To finish her off the Royal Navy dropped depth charges. Not surprisingly there were no survivors from her crew of 34. The U-boat's conning-tower was salvaged a few weeks later and put on display at St Margaret's Hope in South Ronaldsay.

The *UB-116* had originally been built by Blohm & Voss in Hamburg and had only been completed and put into service earlier that year. Measuring 181 feet in length with a beam of 19 feet and a draught of 12 feet she displaced 516 tons on the surface and 641 tons submerged. Driven by her two six-cylinder diesel/electric motors and twin propellers she could achieve a surface speed of 13.6 knots. She had a crew of 34 officers and men and was armed with five 19.7-inch torpedo tubes. Four were situated at the bow and one was located at the stern. On her deck for surface use she had a single 4.1-inch gun fitted. The *UB-116* was salvaged and brought to the surface in 1919 but subsequently re-sunk in her present position at Pan Hope east-north-east of Quoyness. She lay at Pan Hope undisturbed for about 55 years until it was discovered in 1975 that she had a live torpedo in one of her torpedo tubes. The Royal Navy elected to destroy the torpedo with a small controlled explosion. This explosion however detonated the main torpedo warhead and resulted in the *UB-116* being blown to pieces. She did not go down without a fight however. The Royal Navy vessel that was carrying out the operation unfortunately drifted over the site of the *UB-116* just prior to the explosion. When the explosion took place the Royal Navy vessel took a lot of the shock. Windows, crockery and toilet bowls were all smashed by the blast!

Today the *UB-116* lies in about 26 metres of water in a soft sandy bottom. Her remains are well broken up and she is not really recognisable as a U-boat. Torn plates and wreckage litter the sea-bed and amidst these some live shells lie on the sea-bed. There are a number of nets snagged on pieces of debris and in general the wreckage is now being covered by drifting sand.

The *James Barrie*

LOCATION: WIDEWALL BAY, HOXA SOUND

The *James Barrie* was a 666-ton Icelandic steam trawler which had to pass through the Pentland Firth on its way from Hull on 27 March 1969. On her way she ran aground on the Louther Rock and was holed on her port bow. She started to take on water heavily and the crew was forced to abandon her on the rocks. She stayed there for two days and then on 29 March she slid off the rocks and floated off into the Pentland Firth unmanned. She was soon discovered, drifting like a ghost ship, and the Kirkwall lifeboat, the *Grace Paterson Ritchie*, was called out to deal with it. The lifeboat took the *James Barrie* in tow and made for Scapa pier. The *James Barrie* however was shipping too much water and on the way to Scapa it sank. It now lies in Hoxa Sound off Widewall Bay about a mile south of Hoxa Head. The large bronze propeller was successfully salvaged from her a few years ago and now sits by the roadside on Sandwick Road a few miles out of Stromness.

Today the 120-foot long *James Barrie* lies in about 38 metres of water. The least depth over her is about 22 metres. Although the vessel is practically intact its condition is deteriorating and care should be taken on it.

The *F 2*
(Escort vessel)

LOCATION: OFF RYSA LODGE, GUTTER SOUND

The *F 2* was a German Second World War escort vessel similar to a destroyer. She was built at the Germaniawerft shipyard in Kiel and was completed in 1936. Measuring 249 feet in length with a beam of 29 feet and a draught of 11 feet, she displaced 790 tons. The *F 2* was used as an experimental boat and her length was increased to 263 feet and her weight reduced to 756 tons prior to the start of the Second World War when she was converted to a torpedo recovery vessel. At this time four 37mm anti-aircraft guns were removed from her, leaving her with four 20mm anti-aircraft guns. She was equipped with two larger 4.1-inch guns set in single open-backed turrets, one on the bow and one to the stern. She had a crew of 121 officers and men. Driven by twin turbines and two propellers she could achieve speeds of about 28 knots prior to her lengthening in 1939, which reduced her top speed to about 26 knots. She sank at her mooring not far from Lyness in 1946.

Today the *F 2* is a very popular dive. She lies not far from Lyness in Gutter Sound where many of the dive-boats stop for lunch. Being shallower than the German Fleet and close to Lyness she makes a good second or afternoon dive. She lies in about 16 to 18 metres of water on her port side and has a least depth to her hull of about eight metres. The bow to aft of the bridge is intact and in good condition. From the bridge to the stern however, the vessel has been devastated by blasting and is hardly recognisable. Here there is only a mass of tangled pipes, cables, plates and debris. If you descend into this area it can be difficult to orientate yourself and you may find yourself finning away unknowingly from the intact bow area. Finning from the jaws of the bow towards the stern, mooring bollards

The *F 2*   and capstans for the anchors are dotted around the edge of the deck. The winch on her forward deck still holds a reel of steel cable and both anchor cleets are clearly visible. Her anchor chains are run out from an anchor storage box at the bow to the bow anchor cleets and from there hang down to the seabed. Further back and the barrel of her bow 4.1-inch gun looms into view still pointing defiantly out over the bow after all these years. The turret has an open back and the breech and the inner workings of the gun can be examined.

Just behind the 4.1-inch gun-turret there is an open deck hatch with its access ladder still in place, leading into the depths of the bow. Behind the gun-turret sits the bridge. The mainmast which originally ran out from the top of the bridge has fallen on to the sea-bed still intact and has a searchlight platform still in place on it but now half buried in the silty bottom. Amidships there is nothing really recognisable but on the sea-bed to starboard about six metres east of the main wreckage lies what looks like the cogged wracking system for one of her anti-aircraft guns. At her stern the prop-shaft and bearings can still be seen but the propeller itself has been salvaged.

The *F 2* was purchased in 1967 by Metrec Engineering 'to be blown up and salvaged'.

About 24 metres away from the superstructure of the *F 2* lies the 550-ton wooden barge *YC 21* which sank in November 1968 in a storm whilst it was being used in salvage operations on the *F 2*. In its hold can still be found one of the twin 20mm anti-aircraft guns which had been salvaged from the *F 2* before the *YC 21* sank and stowed in its hold.

The *Prudentia*
(Tanker)

LOCATION: HALF A MILE WEST OF JETTY NO. 1, FLOTTA

The *Prudentia* dates from the First World War when she was converted from a small 1,000-ton cargo vessel into a tanker by the installation of three oil tanks in her holds. She sank on 12 January 1916 when she dragged her anchor in bad weather, fouled HMS *Iron Duke*'s buoy and went to the bottom. At the time of her sinking her forward tanks were intact and filled with oil. It was decided to leave her where she was as there was no immediate danger of the oil escaping.

Today the *Prudentia* lies in about 23 metres of water on her port side. She has been lying corroding on the bottom for more than 70 years and is now in a very fragile state and causing a considerable amount of concern. Traces of oil have been leaking from her continuously over recent years, thereby fixing her position. Diving on this wreck should be avoided. The local dive-boat operators will not take you down on it and in any event permission from the owners to dive it would not be granted. It would be all too easy in the present state of the vessel to disturb or damage corroded valves and pipes and this could lead to a major oil spillage.

HMS *Roedean*
(Fleet minesweeper)

LOCATION: ENTRANCE TO LONGHOPE

The 1,094-ton fleet minesweeper HMS *Roedean* was sunk on 13 January 1915 when she hit a mine. She was built by the Naval Construction and Armament Company at Barrow and was completed in 1897. She initially saw service as a Great

The wreck of the *F 2*

Western Railway steamer called the *Roebuck* and for some years up to the outbreak of the First World War plied between Weymouth and the Channel Islands. The Royal Navy took her over in 1914 at the start of hostilities and she was converted into a minesweeper and given her new name HMS *Roedean*. She was 280 feet long with a beam of 34 feet and a draught of 17 feet. She was powered by two coal-fired triple expansion engines and two propellers and had a top speed of 19.5 knots. After her conversion by the Royal Navy she was fitted with two 12-pounder guns.

Today she lies in 15 metres of water in a well sheltered site and makes an excellent second dive. The wreck was blasted in 1953 and 1956 to remove her superstructure and so increase the clearance over her. As a result she is now well broken up and no longer has a recognisable ship's form. A mass of jagged plating, piping, spars and ropes rises up from the seabed to greet divers descending on to her. Her two 15-foot wide boilers can be found in amidst the wreckage amidships with their internal pipework still visible. The drop from the surface to the top of the flattened jumble of wreckage is about

13 metres. Unlike the German Fleet wrecks where the sea-bed is silty, the *Roedean* sits in a very muddy bay and as a result the wreckage is covered with a film of fine mud which is easily stirred up by finning. Clouds of mud billow up from the wreck and ruin the visibility which is normally about eight metres here. As the *Roedean* lies in a sheltered bay there is little current and the mud takes a long time to settle.

The fragmented steel plate main deck cover with its six-foot wide side viewing apertures, which would have sat on top of the bulwark rail, can be seen lying around amidst the wreckage. At the stern area her twin mooring bollards can be seen in the jumble of wreckage with a splined part of the prop shaft visible nearby on the sea-bed.

The Bottle Dive

LOCATION: GUTTER SOUND, OFF LYNESS

Lyness was the main Atlantic HQ for the Royal Navy during the two world wars and until quite recent times was still regularly used by the Royal Navy. As a result, over a long period of time naval ships of all types have lain at anchor here. In the time-honoured tradition of seamen of all nations, anything that was not needed was ditched over the side and now the sea-bed bears silent testimony to this custom. In the middle of Gutter Sound the sea-bed is littered with bottles, crockery, old shell casings and superfluous bits and pieces such as discarded brass syringes. The bottom is a flat silty mixture and bottles and crockery are half embedded in the silt for as far as the eye can see. If you start picking interesting ones up you will soon find that you have more than you can easily carry and it is a case of having to decide which items to bring to the surface and which will have to be left for posterity. Divers have been seen surfacing with their arms full of goodies, unable to dump air as they rise and unable to signal to the surface cover for fear of dropping their haul!

SWANBISTER BAY

This appears to be a scrapyard of parts from several vessels and is a good, safe, sheltered site for novices. The site can be dived by boat, launching at Houghton Bay or from the shore. The wreckage sits in about 10 metres of water and is about 100 metres from the shore. It can be dived at any state of the tide and in most winds except a southerly. Masts, winches and plates are strewn about the sea-bed and in amongst this wreckage sits a cabin, 5.9-inch gun with its turret and barbette. The wreckage rises to about four metres off the sea-bed which is made up of fine, clean sand.

The main wreckage is to be found off the beach on the southmost side of the rocky outcrop to the west side of the Bay. On the north side of this outcrop is a pier and the site is located by lining up a transit from the concrete start of the pier with an old water reservoir on the summit of a nearby hill to the north.

GERMAN E-BOAT
MOTOR TORPEDO BOAT (MTB)
LOCATION: OFF NORTH OF FARA
The remains of a German E-boat dating from the Second World War lie off the north tip of Fara in about 10 metres of water. The hull is well broken up.

HM DRIFTER Imbat
LOCATION: OFF LYNESS PIER
HM Drifter *Imbat* was a small vessel of some 92 tons which collided with another unknown vessel on 4 February 1941 and sank 300 metres to the east of Lyness Pier in Gutter Sound.

She now lies in 14 metres of water.

Diving the Blockships

During both world wars Scapa Flow was used as the main Royal Navy Atlantic anchorage and, to safeguard the British Fleet, attempts were made to block all the main sea entrances into the Flow. Anti-submarine netting was suspended on a floating boom and strung across some of the larger channels into the Flow such as Hoxa Sound. Moving sections much like gates were incorporated into these booms so that they could be opened to allow British vessels to pass. Because of the tidal race in the smaller sounds mining was not feasible. It was not necessary to keep these channels open for navigation like the other larger channels and so 'blockships' were deliberately sunk in them. These blockships were stripped of anything valuable before they were sunk and were mainly made up of damaged vessels and ships that had come to the end of their useful lives. Many of them still lie where they were deliberately sunk but have now become home to a wide variety of marine life. The blockships can be subdivided into two main groups, the 'Burra Sound' blockships and the 'Churchill Barrier' blockships.

As you approach Stromness through Hoy Sound on the mainland ferry from Scrabster you will see Burra Sound off to your right. Eight or more ships have been sunk there over the years and the distinctive bows of the *Inverlane* can clearly be seen jutting upwards high out of the water. Of these eight, only the *Inverlane*, the *Tabarka*, the *Doyle* and *Gobernador Bories* are worth diving today. The others were blown up and dispersed in 1962 by the Royal Navy using 500-pound mines, to minimise the obstruction to shipping through this Sound. There is much wreckage dispersed over a wide area.

The second group of blockships comprise those that were sunk to block the smaller eastern approaches into Scapa Flow namely Kirk Sound, Skerry Sound, East Weddel Sound and Water Sound. Before the Second World War these latter Sounds were navigable channels that posed a real threat to the safety of Royal Navy vessels moored in the Flow. At the start of the Second World War it was thought that the blockships that had been sunk there in the First World War were sufficient to stop German U-boats getting into the Flow. This

The bows of the *Inverlane* jut skywards from Burra Sound

belief was to be proved fatally and tragically flawed when the German U-boat, *U-47* commanded by Gunther Prien, was able to squeeze through the blockships in Kirk Sound and torpedo HMS *Royal Oak* at anchor on 14 October 1939. The blockships in Kirk Sound had been set not nose to tail but parallel and overlapping, leaving a zig-zag path in between them. Prien's attack on the *Royal Oak* was devastating. She filled rapidly with water, turned turtle and sank within five minutes trapping many of her crew inside — 833 British officers and men died in that one attack and Scapa Flow's vulnerability was exposed. Prien was then able to slip back out through the blockships once again to safety. This was Germany's first real success of the war and Churchill determined that there should never be a repeat of this tragedy. He therefore put in hand the construction of the barriers now known simply as the 'Churchill's Barriers'. Using Italian prisoners-of-war he arranged for the 'sounds' or channels to be completely blocked off by huge five to ten ton concrete blocks being set in a line across them. The present road that runs down the islands on the east of Scapa Flow to South Ronaldsay is actually constructed on them and now provides a convenient route for locals and tourists alike.

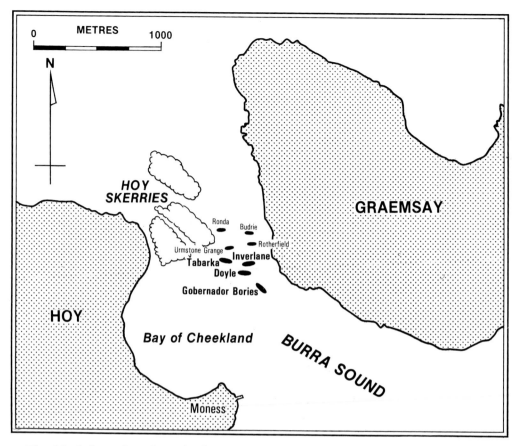

The blockships date from both world wars and have taken the full force of the powerful North Sea storms since then. Many are broken up and others have been blasted or completely removed. The Churchill Barrier blockships now make interesting second dives or night dives and indeed the Burra Sound blockships with an average 30 metre visibility give some of the best diving in the Flow. Some of the blockships on the seaward side of the Barrier No. 4 have become engulfed by the sand that has been driven against them over the years and now form part of a beach that runs along it. Two of them can be reached on foot at low water.

The Burra Sound blockships

The Burra Sound Blockships
The *Inverlane*

The *Inverlane* was built in 1938 at Vegesack in West Germany. She was an 8,900-ton tanker registered in Dublin. She was damaged by a mine off South Shields in 1939 and was split in two. The bow and midships section of her was made watertight and towed to Scapa Flow for use as a blockship and sunk in Burra Sound in 1944. The *Inverlane* is easily recognised as some 100 feet of her bows and hull from the bridge forward jut out of the water at high water and her mast still rises up from her deck. About another 100 feet of her is underneath the water. The common practice is for the dive-boat to moor to the sheltered side of the wreck. It is then possible for divers to go on to the wreck, have a look around and enter the water inside her. If you stop for a moment on her you will sense the whole hull swaying slightly in the current. Although she is still in good condition some of her deck plating is thin in places and the rungs on her ladders are almost rusted through. The wreck feels like a ghost ship and if you peer down into her holds you will see that, even when a fierce tide is running, the water inside her is still and crystal-clear. Although you will dive actually inside the wreck and be protected from the scourge of the current, it is quite safe and not like penetrating a completely enclosed wreck. Since much of the *Inverlane* sticks out of the water, divers will find that the water level is actually beneath the roof in many of the holds and compartments, so that if it becomes necessary to surface there will always be an open area above. The cavernous innards of the hull are lit to some extent by light from above and light filtering through portholes and other openings but a torch is essential. The average depth is about nine metres.

A strong current runs through Burra Sound and this makes the wreck only diveable for about 40 minutes at spring slack waters and for about one and a half hours at neap slack waters. Outside these times you can see the tide ripping around the hull, but the strong current does have its advantages. It scours the wreck free of any silt and sediment and produces some of the best visibility in Scapa Flow. Thirty metres visibility is the norm and this makes this wreck fabulous for underwater photography with no end of willing subjects! The *Inverlane* teems with sea life and the inner workings and pipes have become home for a number of conger eels. Occasionally you may bump into a seal. It is always difficult to judge who gets the biggest shock from such an unexpected face-to-face encounter!

In front of the bows of the *Inverlane* lies the wreckage of another dispersed vessel.

The *Gobernador Bories*

The 2,332-ton iron steamer *Gobernador Bories* predates the

Inverlane, having been built in 1882 at West Hartlepool. She was registered in Punta Arenas, Chile, and was sunk in 1915.

She lies in 16 metres of water, at low water, about 275 metres to the south-east of the *Inverlane*. The least depth over her is about ten metres. Sitting in the same channel as the *Inverlane* she too is affected by the fierce current of about five knots that rages through Burra Sound. Diving is only really possible on her at slack water and neap tides. Again the visibility is excellent, often being up to 30 metres and diving this wreck can be breathtaking. She is a very picturesque wreck and, with Burra Sound's visibility, divers get a diving experience that is almost unknown in Scotland and is more reminiscent of wreck diving in the clear blue seas of some foreign climates. The hull, although broken up in many places, adequately protects divers from the current. The decking in the main has collapsed and inside the hull it is open above. The only times that the current, which runs even at slack water, is felt is during your descent and ascent from the wreck. A firm grip of the shot-line is essential as you go down as it is quite common to find the current driving divers into the horizontal position. Forget trying to surface by rising up holding on to the shot-line or buoy. If the buoy was on the surface when you started your ascent the effect of the current sweeping you downstream will pull the buoy under and you will probably reach it about five metres from the surface. On the other hand, if you have dived this wreck at the wrong time and the current gets a hold of you, you may well find yourself being swept out to sea and being the centre of a rescue. The local skippers will encourage (!) you with stories of divers being picked up from the Atlantic some five miles away but don't let these stories worry you (even though they are true!). The skippers work these waters every day and will make sure that you dive at the right times and pick you up promptly when you surface.

The silt that is so common in the middle of the Flow is swept away from this area by the current and the sea-bed is made up of rocks and clean, white sand. The *Gobernador* sits on her keel in this fine panorama with a slight list to starboard. With such good visibility divers can see large sections of her at any one time and get a real feel for her. Her bow and the starboard side of her hull is practically intact. Inside the open hull, and shielded from the current, the water is still and the only reminder of what is happening around the wreck is the kelp on the top of the hull which will be bent over at right angles by the tidal rip.

Inside the hull it is generally very light but in some of the more intact areas it can be dark and shadowy. Light streams in through openings to give a beautiful contrast. Amidships her two boilers are exposed amongst levels of open decking and the vessel's struts. Finning from here towards the stern there is a large hold area with much wreckage in it. A large winch lies on its back in amongst the debris.

At the stern she regains more of her original shape and ends with her actual stern complete and open and accessible from the inside. From the sea-bed to the deck above in this section is about seven and a half metres and the original stringers are still visible.

The wreck is teeming with life. Fed by the current, filter feeders abound everywhere, covering entire sections of the hull with displays of rich colour. The fish life is plentiful and varied. Divers have been feeding fish on this wreck for years and the fish are used to their presence. Divers are no longer seen as a threat but more as a meal ticket. No sooner will you be down on the wreck than fish will start congregating around you making it abundantly clear that they want to be fed. They will swim just inches away from you waiting for a tasty morsel to be proferred. Some will even let you stroke them. If a goodie is offered to them they are not slow in getting in and will feed from your hand quite happily for some time, spitting out bits of shell through their mouths and gills. Photographers tend to go blue in the face at this stage and disappear in a mass of bubbles as shot after shot is taken. It is quite easy to shoot off a whole spool of film without noticing. Some of the bolder fish will actually follow divers over the wreck waiting for a tasty morsel. Rock wrasse are common and conger eels inhabit some of the deeper holes although I wouldn't advise feeding them!

Of all the wrecks in Scapa Flow this is a completely different experience and will provide some of your most vivid memories of your Scapa Flow diving expedition, not to mention some fantastic photographs. A video camera would produce some startling and dramatic sequences on this wreck.

The *Tabarka*

The *Tabarka* was a 2,624-ton steamer built in 1909 in Rotterdam. She was a single-screw steamer formerly known as the *Pollux* and registered in Rouen. The *Tabarka* was seized at Falmouth in July 1940 by the Royal Navy and taken to Scapa Flow for use as a blockship. She was initially sunk in

Kirk Sound (No. 1 Barrier) where she lay for several years, until 27 July 1944, when she was refloated and moved from her position in Kirk Sound to Burra Sound where she was subsequently resunk.

She lies in 12 metres of water, upside down, immediately to the south of the *Inverlane*. Like the *Gobernador Bories* this wreck is easy to enter and gives protection from the fierce five-knot current that rages through this Sound. The same tremendous visibility and abundance of sea-life that makes Burra Sound one of the most exhilarating dive areas in the Flow makes this wreck another must for Scapa Flow divers.

The *Doyle*

The *Doyle* was a 1,761-ton single-screw steamer built at Troon in 1907 and registered in Belfast. She was sunk in her present location in 1940. She lies to the east of the *Inverlane* in 15 to 17 metres of water and again can only be dived at slack water and neap tides. Like the other wrecks in Burra Sound there is an abundance of sea-life in her with wrasse, lobsters and crabs much in evidence. She sits on an even keel with a noticeable list to port. The starboard side of her hull is intact and gives protection from the fierce tide. The stern section is also relatively intact and her propeller still sits in place. The *Doyle* has two or three open levels of decking to explore. Her two masts lie on the sea-bed to starboard and at the port side of her stern her anchor can also be seen lying there. In the debris and wreckage around this area the steam-driven anchor capstan can be found.

The wreckage in general has a lot of kelp on it, sometimes reminding divers alarmingly of the current that is running even at slack water. Beware as there is a lot of torn netting snagged on parts of this wreck to catch the unwary. Although the maximum depth is in the region of 15 to 17 metres, most of the wreckage lies in about ten metres.

There is a considerable amount of wreckage littering the sea-bed in this whole area. The blasted remnants of several other blockships that were dispersed by the Royal Navy in 1962 include:

The *Budrie*
A 2,252-ton steel single-screw steamer built in Glasgow in 1882. She was registered in Bombay and in her time was called

the *Cannig* and *Golconda*. She was sunk in position in Burra Sound in 1915.

The *Rotherfield*

A 2,831-ton steel single-screw steamer built in West Hartlepool in 1889 and registered in London. She was sunk in position in Burra Sound in 1914.

The *Ronda*

A 1,941-ton steel single-screw steamer built in Sunderland in 1889 and registered in Hull. She was formerly known as the *Rydal Holme* and was sunk in position in 1914.

The *Urmstone Grange*

A 3,423-ton steel single-screw steamer built in Belfast in 1894 and registered in London. She was sunk in the Sound in 1914.

The Churchill Barrier Blockships

The 'Churchill Barriers' run in a southwards line down the east side of Scapa Flow and connect the small islands of Lamb Holm and Glims Holm and the larger islands of Burray and South Ronaldsay to the main land mass of Orkney. There is an easy, pleasant road to drive along by car and it is well worth an afternoon's trip even if you are not contemplating a dive on any of the blockships. The Barriers are made up of huge concrete blocks set in place during the Second World War on the orders of Sir Winston Churchill. The blocks each weigh five to ten tons and are set in a line across each of the channels between these islands. The physical task of filling in the sea to create these barriers was monumental. A vast amount of material had to be dumped in the deeper stretches to make any impression at all. Where was the necessary labour to accomplish this task found? The solution came in the form of hundreds of Italian prisoners-of-war who had been captured during the North Africa campaign. They were taken to Orkney and held in a prisoner-of-war camp on Lamb Holm. During their imprisonment there they came to be well liked and respected and close bonds were formed with the locals and British engineers supervising the construction work. As a reminder of those days you will see on your left as you drive southwards across the small islet of Lamb Holm the small yet famous Italian Chapel constructed by those same prisoners and the remnants of the camp nearby. The original Italian artist, Domenico Chiocchetti, who created the colourful frescoes during his imprisonment on Lamb Holm, returned to Orkney in the 1960s and spent five years lovingly restoring the chapel to its original wartime glory. It is now visited daily by the many tourists who come to Orkney.

The Barriers were Churchill's way of completely sealing off the Flow from attack via the eastern sea-approaches of Kirk Sound, Skerry Sound, East Weddel Sound and Water Sound to prevent a repetition of the tragic torpedoing of the *Royal Oak*. The formation of the Barriers produced a solid impenetrable obstacle to any such attack.

As you drive along the modern road that now runs along the top of the Barriers you will see on either side the rusting wrecks of the blockships. Grim, silent reminders of a war-torn past. Many of the original blockships were removed following the creation of the Barriers as they were no longer needed. Others were dispersed by explosives and the rest were simply left to rot and disintegrate with the elements. Over the years some of the blockships on the seaward east side of the Barriers have become engulfed by the encroaching sand driven on to them by the fierce northern gales. A sandy beach has formed at Barrier No. 4 in Water Sound along which you can walk and examine at first hand, from the shore, some of the Barrier wrecks.

Kirk Sound
(No. 1 Barrier)

As you drive southwards along the A961 you will pass through the small village of St Mary's. Shortly after this you will come to Barrier No. 1 across Kirk Sound. Kirk Sound is mainly about eight metres deep but at its deepest point reaches 15 metres. Being a blocked off channel there is little water movement and the sea-bed is a silty mud mixture. Visibility is about five metres on average. Of the ten blockships that were sunk in this Sound only four remain worth diving. They are:

The *Numidian*

A steel single-screw steamer of 2,890 tons built in Glasgow in 1876 and registered in London. She is the most northerly of the wrecks in this Sound and her remains are now only a jumble of wreckage. Her hull has been almost completely removed. She lies about 60 metres south of the north-west side of the Barrier and so can be dived from a boat or as a shore dive with a snorkel out to the dive site. Fin down the side of

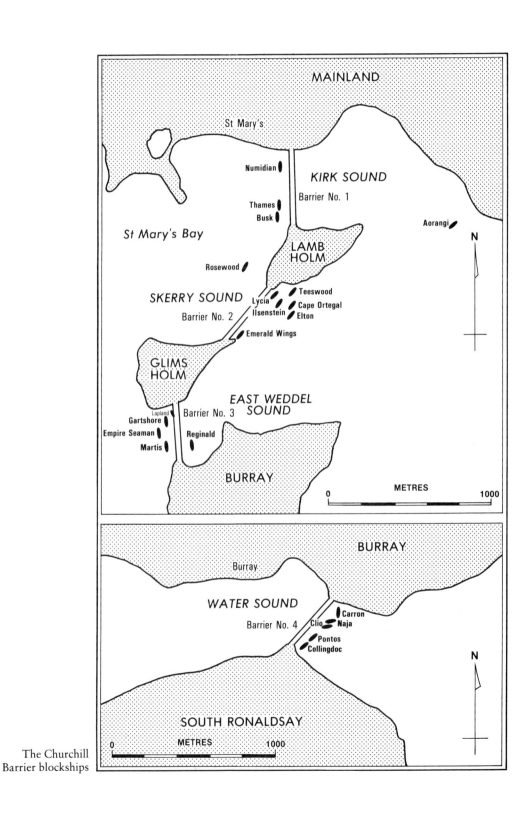

The Churchill
Barrier blockships

the Barrier for 60 metres and then fin out for about 30 metres and you will see the kelp-covered wreckage rising up from the bottom at nine metres. On the way there you will pass the huge 12-metres long cylindrical sheer legs of the block-lifting mechanism which was used to lift the huge five to ten-ton concrete blocks of the Barrier into place. The sheer legs were simply dumped in the sea when their purpose was finished.

Also visible in this area, away from the Barrier itself are more concrete blocks which were used in the first abortive attempts to form a causeway. The main wreckage is made up of layers of collapsed plating lying around on the sea-bed and does not have any recognisable ship's form. The stone blocks used to help sink the blockships can be seen in places. Many large girders and spars jut up from the wreckage to provide convenient footholds for kelp, sea lettuce and sea urchins.

The *Thames*
A 1,327-ton steel single-screw steamer built in Glasgow in 1887 and registered in Grangemouth. She was sunk in her present position in 1914. Her stern has been removed and her hull has been cut down to the main deck to minimise the obstruction to shipping.

The *Aorangi*
A 4,268-ton single-screw steamer built in Glasgow in 1883 and registered in Dunedin, New Zealand. Attempts were made by the Admiralty to sink her in Kirk Sound during the First World War in line with the other blockships there. However she did not sink quickly and drifted with the tide out to sea to the east. She finally sank in her present position some way away from her intended resting place. Being on the east side of the Barrier she makes a good dive if the prevailing wind makes diving on the west side impossible.

The *Busk*
A 367-ton steel single-screw steamer built in 1906 in North Shields and registered at Whitehaven, Cumberland. She broke up in a gale and is now well dispersed.

Skerry Sound
(No. 2 Barrier)

After driving over Kirk Sound the road south continues across

Seaward blockships to the east of Barrier No. 2

Lamb Holm and on to the next channel, Skerry Sound, with Barrier No. 2 dissecting it. Skerry Sound at the Barrier is about nine to ten metres deep and makes an excellent shore dive although it is a long snorkel out to the main wrecks. The distinctive masts and superstructure of the *Elton* sit proud of the water midway along the east side of the Barrier marking the main wreckage area. Consider dropping your weights and bottles at the mid-point of the Barrier and then getting kitted up in either of the car parks at the north and south of the Barrier. Stopping on the Barrier itself is forbidden. It is then possible to walk to your heavier equipment and then clamber down the concrete blocks and enter the water. From here it is a far shorter and less arduous snorkel out to the main wrecks. The depth at the mid-point is about five metres and as you fin away from the Barrier the bottom shelves off gradually to about nine metres at the main wreckage. On the snorkel out you will pass over the scattered and sparse plates and debris of other blockships that have been salvaged over the years. The visibility here on the seaward side of the Barrier is better than on the westward side, averaging ten metres, and there is more sea-life. The bottom is sandy with slabs of stone and deep gullies. The wrecks worth diving in this area are:

The *Elton*

A steel single-screw steamer of 2,461 tons built and registered in West Hartlepool in 1880. She was sunk in her present position in 1915. The midships section remains in fairly good condition and is visible at low water, its mast visible at all times. The stern section has been cut off and removed just aft of the engine room. A large boiler still remains *in situ* and it is possible to swim up the side of it into the engine area. Her funnel lies on the sea-bed hard up against the hull on her starboard side. Just where the stern section has been cut off the prop shaft gearing mechanism can be found lying amid the debris. There is a second section of hull to the front of this section, separated by a gap of about 12 metres. Lying around about the stern section is a considerable amount of ribbed plating, perhaps the remnants of the *Cape Ortegal* or *Rheinfield*.

The *Ilsenstein*

A steel single-screw steamer of 1,508 tons built in Kiel in 1908 and registered in Bremen. She was formerly known as the *Matatua* and was initially sold for breaking up at the end of her useful career. The outbreak of war stopped her breaking up and she was sunk here as a blockship in 1940, replacing the *Cape Ortegal*.

During the war, when materials were scarce, the Italian prisoners-of-war plundered what they could from her and also used her as a convenient stage for fishing. The bows of another blockship, the *Lycia* were high and dry where she had been rammed aground into her allocated position on the north shore under her own steam. The Italians rigged up a gangway from her stern to the stern of the *Ilsenstein*, which was positioned immediately behind her. She was demolished in 1950 but now makes an excellent shore dive for beginners. She is now well broken up and dispersed over a wide area. There are several main areas of wreckage from her and other dispersed blockships in this area. The sea-bed is at eight metres and the height of the wreckage is four metres.

The *Lycia*

A steel single-screw vessel of 2,338 tons built in Port Glasgow in 1924 and registered in Glasgow. She was rammed on to the shore at the north-east end of the Barrier in 1940. The hull has now been cut down to the level of her engine room.

The *Rheinfield*

A steel single-screw steamer of 3,634 tons built in Newcastle in 1893 and once known as the *Ramses*. Registered in Hamburg and sunk in her present position beside the *Elton* in 1914. She is now well broken up.

The F/C *Pontoon*
A crane barge which belonged to Metal Industries Ltd and is still mainly intact but is little more than an empty steel box. Her mooring winches are visible in the middle of the Sound.

The *Teeswood*
Formerly known as the *Westwood*, she was a steamer of 1,589 tons built in 1882. Most of her has been salvaged and removed. Only her engines remain.

The *Cape Ortegal*
A steel single-screw steamer of 4,896 tons built and registered in Glasgow in 1911. She rolled over in a gale and has since broken up. Her remains are visible at low water beside the *Elton* in the middle of the Sound.

The *Rosewood*
A steel single-screw steamer of 1,757 tons built and registered in South Shields in 1889. She was not sunk in the same area as the other blockships but for some reason sank to the west of Lamb Holm and is now almost completely dispersed.

The *Emerald Wings*
A 2,139-ton steel single-screw steamer built in 1920 at Cherbourg and registered in London. She is now well dispersed with a boiler showing at low water.

There are the dispersed remains of several other blockships in this area, amongst others the barge A.C. 6, the *Argyle* and the *Almeria*.

East Weddel Sound
(No. 3 Barrier)

Travelling further southwards along the A961, the road traverses the small islet of Glims Holm and arrives at No. 3 Barrier which dissects East Weddel Sound. At the Barrier, East Weddel Sound is only about four metres deep but the blockships sit in about eight metres of water. Five blockships were sunk in this Sound during the two world wars. In the Great War defensive blockships were positioned during the course of 1914 and 1915. They were the 1,564-ton steamer *Gartshore*, the 1,234-ton steamer *Lapland* and the motor schooner *Reginald*. The later blockships sunk in 1940 were the 1,921-ton steamer *Empire Seaman* and the 2,483-ton steamer *Martis*.

The East Weddel Sound blockships make for excellent shore dives. They are all close in to the Barrier, cutting out the long snorkel as at Barrier Nos. 1 and 2. There is room for car parking at the north side of the Barrier and an easy access to the water. The sea-bed is made up of the familiar silty mixture and is easily stirred up.

On the west side of the Barrier the superstructures of three blockships are visible at low water. They are the *Gartshore*, *Empire Seaman* and *Martis*. Although only a few sections show at low water, as soon as you enter the water from the closer and easier access on the north side, a completely different picture reveals itself. The bottom is littered almost right the way across the Sound with twisted and torn plating and it is difficult to distinguish which wreck it actually comes from. The rudder and prop shaft of the *Empire Seaman* can clearly be seen amidst the chaos. Following the prop shaft southwards, divers are led to the engine room area which, having being blasted open, now has no recognisable ship's shape. It does however still have much of the original engine room equipment lying around. Two large boilers rear up from the sea-bed and a length of a huge camshaft in perfect condition dwarfs any divers who swim past it. Steering gear lies on the sea-bed and the cavernous funnel has collapsed down onto the debris but still has the remnants of the original brass steam whistle in place on it.

The wreckage of the *Gartshore* mingles with that of the *Empire Seaman*. In places the hulls are completely devastated by blasting but elsewhere intact sections of the hull of the *Empire Seaman* rise up from the sea-bed to the surface, giving an idea of the size and dimensions of these vessels. In places the sea-bed has been scoured out from underneath the hull making a traverse through a cave-like passage underneath the hull possible. A large section of the hull of the *Martis* remains intact.

The wreckage is rich in sea-life and is still a scrap merchant's dream with large sections of lead piping sticking out here and there. There are a number of intact portholes with their original toggles still in place on the plating. These are made of cast-iron and are not of any value. They will simply dis-integrate with any attempt to remove them. One large section of the hull's plating lies on the sea-bed and has a tear about 15 metres long on it, presumably as a result of clearance blasting.

The classic schooner lines of the *Reginald* on Barrier No. 3

On the east side of the Barrier although the striking stern hull section of the schooner *Reginald* remains it is in very shallow water and no more than an empty shape.

The *Empire Seaman*

A steel single-screw steamer of 1,921 tons built in Lübeck in 1922 and registered in London. She was originally known as the *Morea* and was a war prize, having been seized by the Royal Navy in 1940. She was taken to Scapa Flow and sunk in East Weddel Sound that same year. Today only her midships section remains, the bow and stern having been cut off and removed along with her engines. The midships area is very broken up and only a few sections of plating are exposed at high water.

The *Lapland*

A steel single-screw steamer of 1,234 tons built in Dundee in 1890 and registered in Liverpool. She was formerly known as the *Dauntless* and the *Ptarmigan*. She lies directly under the Barrier itself and is consequently totally collapsed in. Sections of her can be identified sticking out from underneath the concrete blocks of the Barrier on its north-west side.

The *Martis*

A steel single-screw steamer of 2,483 tons formerly known as the *William Balls*. She was built in South Shields in 1894 and registered in London. Like the *Lapland* her stern and bows have been cut off and removed but sections of her are visible at low water.

The *Reginald*

Perhaps the most striking and visible wreck on this Barrier. The stern section of her hull lying on its starboard side can be seen easily to the east of the Barrier jutting some way out of the water. She now provides a convenient lee to the locals for mooring small boats and for stacking lobster creels. She was a 930-ton iron three-masted motor schooner, built and registered in Glasgow in 1878 and was sunk here in 1915. The dry part of the stern section displays characteristic schooner lines.

The *Gartshore*

An iron single-screw steamer of 1,564 tons built and registered in South Shields. She was sunk as a blockship in 1915.

Water Sound
(No. 4 Barrier)

This is the last of the Churchill Barriers on your journey southwards and connects the island of Burray to South Ronaldsay. At the Barrier, the Sound ranges from four to six metres deep. Of the nine reported blockships that have been sunk here, three date from the First World War and the other six from the Second. Driving across the Barrier you are immediately aware of three prominent wrecks to the east. The *Carron* is substantially intact and sits close to the Barrier itself. Her superstructure has almost all been engulfed by sand that has been driven against the Barrier by the winter storms and now forms part of the beach that runs along the east side. At low water her bridge area is dry and can easily be inspected from the shore. The rest of her lies beneath the sand.

The *Pontos* is perhaps the most dramatic of these wrecks, lying just a short way offshore at the south-east of the Sound. The forward section of her hull with its distinctive mast and lifeboat davits shows above the surface even at high water, marking her position and making this perhaps the most photogenic wreck site of all the Barriers. Nearby the concrete-lined bridge and bow of the steamer *Collingdoc* are firmly embedded in the sand at the south-east of the Barrier. At low

The remnants of the *Carron* lie embedded in the sand at Barrier No. 4

water her bows are dry and it is possible to clamber up and see inside the bridge. The deck still has some of its original wooden planking in place despite the years exposed to the elements and her anchor winching gear remains in good condition. It is possible with some effort and care to get inside the bridge although there is a big hole in the middle of it. From here you can get some tremendous photos of the *Pontos* framed by the bridge portholes of the *Collingdoc*. From the deck again you can get some good views of the *Pontos* with the rusted ladders and framework of the *Collingdoc* in the foreground to give contrast.

The *Carron*

A 1,017-ton single-screw steel steamer formerly known as the *Glasgow*. She was built in Dundee in 1894 and registered in Grangemouth. She was laid as a blockship in this Sound in 1940. Although she is substantially intact she is now mainly buried in the sand at the north-east side of the Barrier. Only a small section of her superstructure is exposed today and is dry at low water. Her general shape can be made out at low water from her ribs which run out to sea and into the sand. Her stern mast has collapsed across the hull.

The *Collingdoc*

A 1,780-ton steel single-screw steamer built in 1925 in Hill-on-Tees and registered in Fort William, Ontario, Canada. She saw many years service as a Great Lakes steamer before being taken over by the Admiralty and sunk in her present position in 1942. She is well embedded in the sand at the south-east corner of the Barrier with her bridge and bow section rising out of the beach and being dry at low water. Her bridge is set right at the bows in a style common to many inland steamers. Her bridge is still lined with concrete which was a cheap yet effective way of armouring it. Her anchor winch still sits on her wood-lined deck.

The *Collingdoc* lies embedded in the sand with the *Pontos* in the background

The *Lorne*

A 1,186-ton single-screw steamer built in Hull in 1873 and registered in Southampton. She was sunk in her present position to the east of the *Clio* in 1915. Explosives were used to disperse her some time ago and she is now broken up although a large section of her hull is still to be found lying near the *Clio*.

The *Pontos* photographed from the *Collingdoc*

The *Gondolier*

A 173-ton paddle-steamer built and registered in Glasgow in 1866. She saw service with David MacBrayne Limited, the Caledonian Canal Service, before sinking to the south-east of the Barrier in 1940.

The *Juniata*

A twin-screw steel motor tanker built in Sunderland in 1918 and registered in London. She lies to the north-east of the Barrier where she was sunk in 1940.

The *Pontos*

A steel single-screw steamer of 3,265 tons built in Glasgow in 1891 and registered in Andros, Greece. She was formerly known as the *St John City* and the *Clan MacNab*. She rests to the south-east of the Sound about 12 metres offshore where she was sunk in 1914. She is clearly visible, the forward section of her hull with its distinctive tall mast still standing proudly despite the ravages of nearly 80 years of Atlantic storms. Just aft of the mast can be seen two empty lifeboat davits. It is an easy snorkel out to her with the bottom shelving off quite rapidly to the depth she sits in of about ten metres. The wreck is well corroded but substantially intact. She has many entrances into her innards and is open in many places to the surface. A lot of light filters down through openings in her deck creating shadows and shafts of sunshine. She is a good shore or second dive.

The *Clio*

A single-screw steel steamer of 2,733 tons built in Hartlepool in 1889 and registered in Hull. She is situated in the middle of the Sound with her boilers and engines exposed at high water. She was sunk in her defensive position in 1914.

The *Naja*

A concrete barge sunk in 1939 immediately to the north of the *Clio*.

Scapa's War Graves—the Forbidden Wrecks

The Tragedy of the *Royal Oak*
14 October 1939

A solitary green Admiralty wreck-buoy marks the site of the sinking of the *Royal Oak* not far from the small port of Scapa. On a calm day a long slick of diesel oil can be seen above the wreck. Small droplets of oil still rise up from the wreck to burst on the surface in a kaleidoscope of colour. It is hard on tranquil days to believe that such a tragic event could have occurred here so close to Scapa and the shore. Many of the 833 men who died on this day were trapped inside the vessel as it heeled over. Others died of exposure in the freezing winter waters.

The *Royal Oak* was commissioned in 1916 and served with distinction at the Battle of Jutland, claiming two hits. Two years later she sailed down the Pentland Firth to form part of the British force that led the German High Seas Fleet into internment at Scapa Flow. She was more than an eighth of a mile (660 feet) long and had a beam of 102 feet. She displaced 29,150 tons and was protected by a 13-inch armoured belt from her main deck all the way down to five feet beneath the water-line. Further precaution against airborne attack was a layer of three-inch steel on each of her three main decks, each of which was 1,000 feet long. Below her armoured belt she was protected by two huge torpedo blisters, one on either side. These enormous tubeless watertight blisters boosted her buoyancy and lessened her tendency to roll. More importantly they formed a false hull which it was hoped would cause any torpedo to explode prematurely without causing any damage to the main hull. If she was a mighty ship in the First World War, 23 years later she was a slow, old ship by comparison with the Fleet's newer vessels. The *Royal Oak* could do no

The *Royal Oak*
(IWM)

more than 21 knots and so could not keep up with the main body of the Fleet. She carried eight massive 15-inch guns in four turrets each of which in turn held 208 shells. Her guns were so powerful that they could hurl 2,000 one pound shells at enemy vessels 13 miles away.

War had been declared only six weeks earlier and there was still a certain amount of disbelief. The war seemed far away and unreal. Scapa Flow was practically deserted. The Admiralty knew that Scapa Flow was no longer the safe impregnable anchorage it had been in the First World War. Its defences had either rusted away or been removed. As a consequence the Home Fleet was being rotated from one insecure base to another to avoid attack. Because the main threat was considered to be from the air the *Royal Oak* had been left moored near Scapa as a floating anti-aircraft platform where her powerful guns could give protection to nearby Kirkwall and the surrounding area.

At precisely midnight on 13 October the watches had changed over. Most of the crew had turned in early after their recent stormy journey home, glad to be back in the relative safety of Scapa Flow. To them the *Royal Oak* was solid,

Starboard view of
the *Royal Oak*
(IWM)

secure and unsinkable. Scapa Flow was completely blacked out and the riding lights of the *Royal Oak* and the only other vessel near her, *Pegasus*, two miles off to port, had been painted blue in accordance with blackout regulations. They were only visible from about 180 metres. Light-excluding ventilators had been fitted to the portholes instead of the usual glass scuttles. Whilst preventing light escaping they were not waterproof and if submerged, water would gush through them flooding the vessel. In the dark the watches could dimly make out the barren and deserted cliffs about half a mile away, silhouetted against the starlit night sky. The black water was 48°F, cold enough to shock and numb a man within minutes. The fishing drifter *Daisy II*, which had been busy earlier that day ferrying liberty parties ashore, was now tied up alongside the *Royal Oak*. It was a calm, peaceful scene.

At 1.04 a.m. on 14 October the silence was shattered by an explosion forward. Most of the crew assumed that the explosion was the result of a bomb dropped from an aircraft that had glided overhead with its engines off as the watches had not seen the tell-tale water spout and cascade of water that marks a torpedo hit on a ship. Hard on the heels of the explosion came a thunderous roar and the anchor chains, leading from a point on the centre-line of the vessel well back from the bow, were seen to be running out freely. About 200 men of the crew of 1,200 were on watch. Most of those below were awakened by the explosion and roar of the anchor chains. Some started to throw on their clothes and make their way above. To others more distant from the explosion the explosion seemed remote and of a minor nature. No alarm rattles sounded to warn them and many assumed it was a small internal explosion and went back to sleep. On deck there was no sign that anything was wrong. The explosion had only seemed violent to those near it, some of whom had been pitched from their hammocks by its force. What was alarming was that the whole 29,150 tons of the *Royal Oak* had shaken and that pointed to something a lot more serious. There was however no alteration to the trim of the ship so if a hole had been blown in her hull then it must have been well forward beyond the collision bulkhead. It was impossible to hold a hand over the vents leading to the spaces near the source of the explosion because of the pressure of air being forced out by the water that was now flooding into the damaged area.

Shortly afterwards, whilst everyone was still speculating about the explosion, there was a dull thump and those on deck saw a great column of spray rise up the side of the ship as high as the spotting top. The ship shuddered violently and lamp fittings and bulkheads shook. Men in the lower decks near this explosion were pitched from their hammocks and water started pouring in below decks. The crew fled in the face of this torrent which swept their belongings with it.

Less than a minute later there were two almost simultaneous thumps. It may only have been one explosion. This time there was no spray but a large cloud of black smoke from atomised oil fuel started to form. The ship started to heel over quickly to starboard, shaking and shuddering as the weight of inrushing water altered her trim. The starboard engine room and No. 1 boiler room had been blasted into chaos and torn open to the cruel sea.

Suddenly there was a final explosion right under the Marines' mess deck and the *Royal Oak* heeled over to about 15 degrees. In minutes the 60 or so light-excluding ventilators along her starboard side would be submerged, allowing water to flood in and hasten her doom. On this last explosion the lighting system was destroyed and all the decks below were flung into a terrifying darkness. The broadcasting system was also destroyed and no orders could be sent to the men below. Hundreds of terrified men struggled to find a way above, losing their sense of direction in the passages and cross passages, running into dead ends and colliding with each other. They knew what was now inevitable. The *Royal Oak* was going to turn turtle. This final explosion had set an after magazine on fire and burning cordite gas swept through the vents. Orange pillars of flame soared up through open hatches and men fled before it. Some could not escape it and were engulfed, being turned into human torches. The men's hammocks glowed red in the darkness, smouldering. Some, like flaming cocoons, still held their former occupants in them. Once the flame had reached open air and dissipated it left a suffocating gas that left men coughing and gasping for air. In the confusion some men thought they were under airborne attack and made their way below decks as they had been trained, to get below the protection of the armoured deck. It was the wrong way to go.

The *Royal Oak* continued her remorseless heel over to starboard and as the angle of her decks increased so it became more difficult to open the heavy doors inside. Crowds of men struggled in the darkness to climb up ladders to safety. Gear and belongings started to roll down the increasing incline of the decks. Some water-tight doors were now slamming shut, preventing escape. As the sea of humanity surged and fought to find a way out, the rising fear of becoming trapped inside the ship became overwhelming.

The *Royal Oak* was now heeled over at an angle of 45 degrees and the water flooded in, trapping the men who had not made good their escape. The bulk of the 1,200 men only had about five minutes to find one of the few openings on to the upper decks and funnel themselves out through the crush. Some were able to unscrew the light-excluding ventilators and escape through them. Most however were still in the ship when it finally heeled over.

Above decks men were throwing everything that would float into the water and then walking down the now exposed side of the hull to jump into the water. Beneath their very feet panic and terror reigned. The *Royal Oak*'s great guns swung slowly around in their turrets to point down towards the water. There was a final explosion from the battleship and it gave a great lurch throwing about the men on its side. Many of them were badly burnt. Their hair had been burnt off and skin hung off them in sheets. They felt little pain however. Their immediate concern was to get off the *Royal Oak* and away from her before the suction carried them down. The pain would come later. Men had boarded the drifter *Daisy II* moored alongside. With the tilt of the *Royal Oak* the port torpedo blister rose up underneath *Daisy* lifting her bows about seven to eight metres out of the water. With her engines at full astern she struggled to free herself. Then with a mighty roar she slid off and as soon as her engines were stopped she started picking up survivors.

The *Royal Oak* gave a final lurch then, like a great whale, rolled right over so that her fighting top was submerged. As she went over there was a tremendous crashing noise as racks of shells and other gear fell about inside her. Still trapped inside her were nearly 800 men.

As the *Royal Oak* went over Sick Berth Attendant Bendall had been attempting to get through a porthole in the pantry of the Petty Officers' mess. Everything turned upside down for him and he was thrown back into the compartment. Water poured in through the open porthole. Luckily a bubble of air had been trapped and the remorseless rise of the water level inside the cabin stopped. Bendall found himself with his head touching the former floor and the only means of escape was an open porthole one and a half metres below him in the dark oily water. The surface of Scapa Flow was 20 metres above him and the upturned hull of the *Royal Oak*, although still afloat was settling into the water every second. Bendall duck-dived to find the porthole, failed and surfaced gasping for air. He duckdived again, couldn't find it and surfaced to where the air pocket should have been. It had gone. With the air in his lungs exhausted he writhed about frantically searching for the porthole and suddenly found himself outside the sub-merged hull and rising up through the black water. He was the last man to get out alive from the *Royal Oak*.

At the surface, air bubbled up the sides of the hull as it was forced out by the inrushing water. A few men stood on top silhouetted in the searchlight from the *Pegasus*. Slowly the *Royal Oak* sank from sight taking the 800 men inside down with her. She sank through the water until her main mast and fighting top struck the sea-bed in almost 30 metres of water. Her 29,150 tons following down on top drove much of her superstructure into the sandy bottom. Oil poured from the submerged vessel creating slicks many feet thick.

On Sunday 15 October diving operations began on the wreck. Nets had been draped over the sunken vessel to catch any bodies floating out of it. The sight that greeted divers descending into the gloom was macabre. Bodies were jammed half in and half out of portholes caught in a last frantic effort to get out. In the hull there were more corpses, some pinned by gear that had moved about as the ship tilted. On the sea-bed divers encountered drowned crew members drifting

THIS MARKS
THE WRECK OF
H.M.S. ROYAL OAK
AND THE GRAVE OF
HER CREW. RESPECT
THEIR RESTING PLACE
UNAUTHORISED DIVING
PROHIBITED

The inscription on the *Royal Oak* wreck buoy

more or less upright in the slight current. It was said that divers came up crazed with horror at what they had seen below in the wreck.

Today the 29,150 ton wreck of the *Royal Oak* lies in almost 30 metres of water resting on her port side with her inverted deck at an angle of 45 degrees. Her massive main hull is largely intact and rises up to about five metres below the surface. On a still clear day it is easily visible from the surface although her shallowest areas have a thick covering of kelp. The whale-back of her upturned hull shelves off steeply into the depths and then stops abruptly at about 16 metres, where the decking starts to run under the hull itself into a shadowy darkness. From here it is a sheer drop of 15 metres to the sea-bed. Her visible superstructure shows considerable impact damage from the initial contact with the sea-bed. Her gun-turrets are accessible under the hull and the eight-foot wide breeches are clearly visible. The barrels are, however, well embedded in the sea-bed. An excellent detailed description of the present condition of the wreck with superb photographs can be found in *Exploring Shipwrecks* by Keith Morris and Peter Rowlands.

The Sinking of the *Hampshire* and the Death of Lord Kitchener
5 June 1916

The 10,850-ton armoured cruiser *Hampshire* (IWM)

The name of one of Britain's greatest war heroes, Lord Kitchener, will forever be linked with Orkney. For it was here off the bleak 60-metre cliffs of Marwick Head on the west coast, that the 10,850 ton armoured battle cruiser *Hampshire* carrying Lord Kitchener on a voyage to Russia struck a mine and sank. At 450 feet long, the *Hampshire* was a strong, powerful warship well suited to the ill-fated voyage through the colossal seas around the north cape of Norway to the port of Archangel in northern Russia. Of the crew of 655 officers and men, and Lord Kitchener and his staff, only 12 would survive. The wreck of the *Hampshire* is a war grave and cannot be dived. It lies in 60 metres of water about one and a half miles off Marwick Head. High on the nearby desolate cliffs at Marwick Head stands the tall, solitary Kitchener Memorial which marks the nearest land point to the site of the sinking.

Lord Kitchener had been the driving force behind Britain's

Lord Kitchener
(IWM)

Kitchener's
famous recruiting
poster (IWM)

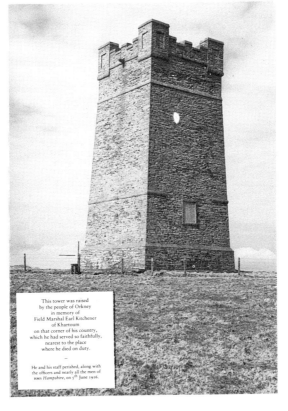

This tower was raised
by the people of Orkney
in memory of
Field Marshal Earl Kitchener
of Khartoum
on that corner of his country,
which he had served so faithfully,
nearest to the place
where he died on duty.

—

He and his staff perished, along with
the officers and nearly all the men of
HMS *Hampshire*, on 5th June 1916.

The
Kitchener Memorial
atop the cliffs at
Marwick Head with
(inset) a
commemorative
plaque

recruitment campaign in the early years of the War with his famous 'YOUR COUNTRY NEEDS YOU' poster. By 1916 the hand of fate had turned against him and he was being openly criticised for his war tactics and beliefs. In the years following his death a bitter controversy raged about the sinking. Was it really a mine as the official explanation bore out or was it a bomb planted by German, Irish or even British saboteurs? Great play was made of the fact that the Stromness lifeboat had not put to sea to pick up survivors and that locals trying to get to the scene to help in a shore search were turned back at bayonet point.

The wreck of the *Hampshire* was surveyed in 1977 and 1983 when its 43-ton bronze propeller and drive shaft were illegally salvaged. The evidence from these surveys confirms the Admiralty version that the *Hampshire* struck a mine. The plating at the bow at the site of the explosion was blown inwards and not outwards as one would expect with an internal explosion.

Russian ineptitude in organising their own affairs and the vast sums of money being expended by Britain in funding the Russian war effort had led to the idea of Lord Kitchener being sent to Russia to impress on the Russians that Britain was not a bottomless fund of munitions and to discuss common war aims and strategy. At the beginning of June 1916 Kitchener travelled up to Thurso and crossed the stormy Pentland Firth from Thurso to Scapa Flow in the destroyer HMS *Oak*. He had never been a good sailor and was unwell during the crossing. He was received by Admiral Jellicoe and the flag officers of the British Grand Fleet. At lunch he listened with interest as they recounted their exploits in the Battle of Jutland which had taken place only a few days earlier.

The *Hampshire* received her sailing orders on 4 June. She was directed to proceed to Archangel in northern Russia, a journey of 1,649 miles. She was to pass up the east side of Orkney on a route that was regularly swept for mines and to maintain a speed of not less than 18 knots up to Lat. 62°N. She was to pass midway between the Shetlands and Orkney and keep not less than 200 miles from the Norwegian coast on her journey north. She would have a protective screen of two destroyer escorts as far north as Lat. 62°N and from there on she would proceed alone at 16 knots, zig-zagging to avoid torpedo attack.

On 5 June, however, the weather worsened and by the afternoon a gale was blowing from the north-east. A heavy sea was running along the east coast, making mine sweeping

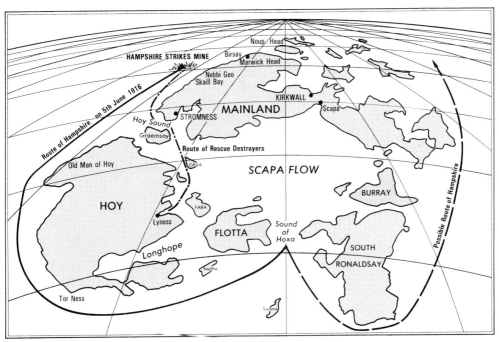

The available routes north from Scapa Flow

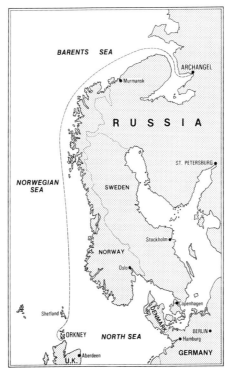

Chart showing Kitchener's
proposed route to
Archangel

difficult. The Admiralty felt that the heavy sea would make it difficult for the *Hampshire*'s two destroyer escorts to keep up with the bigger and more powerful cruiser. The plan was therefore changed and it was decided to send the *Hampshire* by one of the western routes. Of the two available routes it was decided to use the route set up in January 1916 which went past Hoy. This route was not regularly swept for mines but it was thought that no German mine-layer would dare to operate this close to the heavily protected British base. Admiral Jellicoe and his staff felt that with a north-easterly wind this route would give the destroyers a lee and enable them to keep up with the *Hampshire*.

The fateful decision having been made, the *Hampshire* slipped her mooring buoy and cleared the harbour at about 4.40 p.m. She steamed out of the Flow through Hoxa Sound to the south and then turned westwards into the stormy weather of the Pentland Firth to rendezvous with her escort destroyers, *Victor* and *Unity* off Tor Ness on the south-west of Hoy. The two destroyers fell into line behind the *Hampshire*.

Jellicoe and his aides had misinterpreted the prevailing weather conditions for, within an hour, the storm centre had passed overhead and the wind backed sharply to the north-west. The conditions now facing the *Hampshire* and her escorts were exactly the opposite of what had been predicted. At 6.05 p.m. the smaller and less powerful destroyer *Victor* signalled that she could only maintain 15 knots. At 6.10 p.m. the *Unity* signalled that she could only maintain 12 knots and then at 6.18 p.m. signalled that she could only make 10 knots. At 6.20 p.m. the *Hampshire* signalled that she should return to base. Shortly after this the *Victor* signalled that she could not maintain any speed greater than 12 knots and so at 6.30 p.m. the *Hampshire* signalled that the *Victor* should also return to base. The destroyers were off the entrance to Hoy Sound when they turned for home. The *Hampshire* went on alone fighting the fury of the force nine gale.

It was 7.40 p.m. An hour had passed in which the *Hampshire* had struggled to make progress into the eye of the storm. She dipped and crashed in the raging seas and the bow splash billowed over her forecastle. She was only making 13.5 knots and was about one and a half miles from shore between Marwick Head and the Brough of Birsay. Suddenly a rumbling explosion shook the whole ship tearing a huge hole in her keel between her bows and the bridge. The helm jammed and the lights gradually went out as the power failed. With no power she could not make radio contact with the shore to call for assistance. The explosion seemed to be on the port side just forward of the bridge and according to survivors seemed to tear the heart right out of the ship. She immediately began to settle into the water. A cloud of brown, suffocating smoke poured up from the stoker's mess forward making it difficult to see on the bridge. Most of the crew were below and most of the hatches were battened down and shored up for the night. The men began to knock out the wedges and proceed to their stations. The after-hatch to the quarter-deck was open and as the crew streamed aft away from the explosion an officer was heard to call out 'Make way for Lord Kitchener'. He passed by, clad in a greatcoat, and went up the after-hatch, just in front of one of the few survivors. He was last seen standing on the deck of the *Hampshire* and it can only be assumed that he went down with the ship.

The cruiser was settling quickly into the water by the bows. There was no power to work the lifeboat derricks and none of the larger boats was able to be hoisted out. Those smaller boats that were lowered into the water were smashed to pieces against the side of the *Hampshire* by the force of the storm. Not a single survivor saw any boat get clear away from the ship. A number of men took their places in the large boom boats which could not be lowered in the hope that as the ship went down these boats would float off. They were carried down with the *Hampshire* by the suction she created.

At about 7.50 p.m., only 10 to 15 minutes after striking the mine, she went down bows first, heeling over to starboard. Smoke and flame belched from just behind the bridge. Her stern lifted slowly out of the water and her propellers were seen clear of the water still revolving slowly as she went under.

Only three oval, cork and wood Carley rafts got away from the sinking ship, one of which had only six men in it. Faced with the severe conditions it was flung over twice, jettisoning the men into the sea. Only two men were alive when it reached the safety of Skaill Bay. There were 40 to 50 men on the second larger Carley raft. It made the shore just north of Skaill Bay at 1.15 a.m. Only four of its occupants had survived the journey. The third Carley raft had about 40 men in it when it left the sinking ship. It picked up about another 30 from the water. It was very cold and the men were drenched. With the wind chill, most of the men were soon suffering from exposure, losing consciousness or foaming slightly at the mouth. Most never regained consciousness. At 1 a.m. it finally surged up on to the rocks in a small creek called Nebbi Geo, half a mile north of Skaill Bay. There were only six men left alive in it.

The subsequent search at sea located 13 mines in the vicinity of the wreck site, laid at a depth of seven to nine metres. They were deep enough to let smaller vessels such as fishing boats or mine-sweepers sail over the top of them and designed to catch the bigger vessels. A spread of 22 mines had been laid by *U-75* on 29 May as part of the German master plan for the Battle of Jutland four days earlier. The German High Seas Fleet had been put to sea to lure the British Grand Fleet out of its safe anchorage at Scapa Flow. German U-boats were to lie in wait for it. Three mine-laying U-boats including the *U-75* were sent out to mine the likely areas the British Fleet would pass and German intelligence was aware of the route used by the *Hampshire*. It is ironic that *U-75* sailed from Germany two days before Jellicoe even knew of Lord Kitchener's proposed journey. With the death of Lord Kitchener the Germans had unintentionally scored an immense victory which struck at the hearts of the British people. He may have been out of favour but he was still a legend in his own lifetime. The great liberatoi of the Sudan from Muolim aggression, he had led the relief force which had lifted the Maddi's seige of Khartoum in an attempt to save that other hero of the British Empire, General Gordon. He had quelled the Boer uprising in South Africa and on his return home had been given a rapturous and patriotic welcome. It was thus natural that at the outbreak of the Great War Britain should have turned to its supreme warlord for leadership and appointed him Secretary of State for War. His loss was an untimely and bitter blow for the nation.

HMS *Vanguard*

On the night of 9 July 1917 the battleship *Vanguard* lay at anchor about one mile north-north-east of Flotta with the *Royal Oak* alongside. In one cataclysmic magazine explosion she was completely destroyed in seconds. Witnesses spoke of hearing the classic whoosh-bang of a magazine explosion. Unstable cordite had exploded initially and this set off the main magazine. More than 700 men were killed and of the entire ship's complement only one officer and two ratings survived. Captain R. F. Nichols who was in command of the *Royal Oak* at the time it was torpedoed in the Flow in 1939, had been a young midshipman on the *Vanguard*. He lived to

The sheer cliffs at Marwick Head

command the *Royal Oak* because on the night the *Vanguard* exploded he had been attending a concert party presented by *Royal Oak* sailors on the theatre ship *Gourko*. The show had lasted longer than intended and he had missed his boat back to the doomed *Vanguard*.

The *Vanguard* was a mighty ship displacing 19,560 tons. She was built by Vickers at Barrow and completed in February 1910. At 536 feet long with a beam of 84 feet and a draught of 29 feet, she was powered by four Parsons oil-fired turbines which drove her four propellers and pushed her to achieve speeds of 22 knots. She was protected by 10-inch main belt armour plating, 11 inches on her gun-turrets and three inches on her lower armoured deck. Her forward control tower had ten inches of armour plating and her aft eight inches.

She boasted ten 12-inch guns set in pairs in five turrets at the time of her commissioning. She also had 12 4-inch guns and four 8-pounders. Three submerged 18-inch torpedo tubes, two at the bow and one at the stern added to her fighting capability. She had a ship's complement of 758 officers and men.

Today the wreck of the *Vanguard* sits in 34 metres of water on a silty, muddy bottom. The vessel was devastated by the magazine explosion and reminders of that destruction are everywhere. Jagged plates and spars cover the sea-bed in all directions and live ammunition can still be found in amongst the debris. The bow section with its original wooden deck planking is still recognisable pointing upwards. Mooring bollards and steam-driven anchor capstans are still in place alongside the remnants of mushroom-topped deck ventilators. Piles of rope are heaped on top of some sections. Only a 60-foot section of her stern remains intact. In recent years the *Vanguard* has been classified as a war grave and no diving is permitted on her.

Travel, Accommodation and Dive-Boat Charters

1. *GETTING THERE*

Scapa Flow is situated at the most northerly tip of mainland Scotland, so for the majority of divers who visit it travel costs will be a significant expense to consider. For Scottish divers the cost will not be prohibitive and a few hours driving will see you safely to the ferry terminal to Orkney at Scrabster, near Thurso. For others coming from further afield transport may well be one of the most significant expenses. The overall cost of the expedition will fall into four major categories namely, (i) transport, (ii) hire of the dive-boat, (iii) accommodation and (iv) subsistence. This chapter gives some background information on travel and accommodation. If you require any further assistance then contact the Orkney Tourist Board at either (0856) 2856 or 850716.

(a) *By Land*

The main land route to Orkney by road or rail centres on getting to Scrabster on the north coast of mainland Scotland. Scrabster is a small port about two miles west of Thurso and it is from here that you will catch the P & O ferry to the town of Stromness in Scapa Flow itself. Most traffic going north to Orkney converges at Inverness and crosses the Beauly Firth on the impressive Kessock Bridge to the Black Isle. From there take the A9 (which actually starts as far south as Perth) and follow it as it winds its way north, across the Cromarty Firth and then as it meanders along the side of the Dornoch Firth and then further north, hugging the east coast. The scenery is quite breathtaking in places and the drive north is quiet and relaxing. Turn off the A9 at Latheron and continue on the A895 and subsequently on the A882 to Thurso and on to Scrabster. The journey north to Scrabster from Inverness will take two to three hours' driving depending on road conditions.

Coach services from England may require overnight stops at Glasgow, Edinburgh or Inverness on the way to Wick or Thurso. The services are modern and comfortable and local coaches generally connect with ferry sailings. For further information contact your local tourist office or the following services.

HIGHLAND OMNIBUSES	Telephone Inverness (0463) 237575
RAPSON'S COACHES	Telephone Dingwall (0349) 884466
SCOTTISH CITY LINK COACHES	Telephone Glasgow (041) 332 9191
STAGECOACH	Telephone Perth (0738) 33481

If you are travelling by rail take British Rail links to Inverness where a connection to Thurso or Wick can be taken. Some routes from England may require an additional change at Edinburgh or Glasgow. Indeed, in Glasgow it may even be necessary to change stations. Check on this with your local British Rail station when planning your route. From Thurso or Wick buses will take you to the ferry terminal at Scrabster.

(b) *By Sea*

(i) *Scrabster to Stromness*

P & O's fully stabilised roll on/roll off ferry sails from Scrabster to Stromness each day (except Sundays) at 12 noon. Extra sailings are laid on, from 6 May to 26 October, and sailings on Sundays are available in July and August. If you are taking a vehicle across you must be there at least one hour before sailing. (There is a long-stay car park at the ferry terminal for those wanting to cut costs and leave their vehicle on the mainland.) The charge for an average-sized car is upwards of £50 return and in addition each passenger must pay a separate charge. It is expensive to take an inflatable across as, with its trailer, it takes up the same space as a car and is charged accordingly, doubling the cost. Consider taking a minibus across or arrange to hire one on Orkney. This will give transport for a large number of people on Orkney and maximises the number of people who can cross for the one vehicle payment. It may also be worth your while leaving your car at the long-stay car-park and hiring a car on Orkney for a few days to have some mobility for sightseeing.

The ferry from Scrabster crosses the Pentland Firth and then runs up the west coast of Orkney passing close by the Old Man Of Hoy. Have your camera at the ready for the superb views of the Old Man and the sheer cliffs that form the west coast of Orkney. It takes two hours or more for the ferry to reach Stromness, depending on the weather conditions. The Pentland Firth can be one of the roughest pieces of water around the British coast. If you have not yet got your sea legs, position yourself near some of the sick bags that are tactfully placed around the lounges and stay close to one of the exits to the deck. Check out the way the wind is blowing at an early stage . . . it may pay dividends later!

There is also one sailing from Stromness to Scrabster each day (barring Sundays) at 8.45 a.m. and the same rules apply about checking in early. Additional sailings are available during the peak times from May to October as above.

To book, telephone Stromness (0856) 850655 or Aberdeen (0224) 572615.

(ii) *John O' Groats to Burwick*

There is a shorter ferry trip run by Thomas & Bews from John O' Groats to Burwick on the southern tip of South Ronaldsay, a journey of about 40 minutes. This is a passenger-only service and cars cannot be taken across. The service operates between 29 April and 24 September with daily departures from John O' Groats at 9 a.m. and 6 p.m. and from Burwick at 9.50 a.m. and 6.45 p.m. In addition in July and August, from Monday to Saturday there are extra sailings leaving John O' Groats at 10.30 a.m. and 4 p.m. and departing Burwick at 11.30 a.m. and 5 p.m. This ferry would be ideal if you are staying near Burray from where a lot of diving is done. If you are staying at Stromness then this ferry is impracticable unless you have transport on South Ronaldsay organised.

To book, telephone Thomas & Bews at John O' Groats (0955) 81353.

(iii) *Aberdeen to Stromness*

It is possible to travel to Orkney by P & O's ferry the *St Sunniva* which leaves Aberdeen at 12 a.m. on Saturdays arriving Stromness at 8 p.m.

To book, telephone P & O at (0856) 850655 or (0224) 572615.

(iv) *Gill's Bay to Burwick*

Orkney Ferries proposed new roll on/roll off ferry service will run from Gill's Bay on the west of John O' Groats to Burwick in South Ronaldsay. The ferry will leave on the hour from Burwick at 6 a.m. and from Gill's Bay at 7 a.m., and alternatively by the hour until the final departure time from Gill's Bay at 9 p.m.

To enquire for further details telephone Burwick (0856) 83343 or Kirkwall (0856) 5300.

(c) *By Air*

Both British Airways and Loganair have regular daily flights to Kirkwall airport. The costs vary greatly and there are special deals available on enquiry. If you want to take the easy way of getting to Orkney and avoid all the hours of travel and inconvenience then you should get in touch with your local airport, the Orkney Tourist Board or use the undernoted numbers. Remember that most of the dive-boats have bottles and weights provided as part of their all-in dive package so it will not be essential to take your own. Check with the dive-boat operator beforehand.

BRITISH AIRWAYS: Kirkwall (0856) 3359, Inverness (0463) 239871, Aberdeen (0224) 574281, Glasgow (041) 332 9666, Edinburgh (031) 225 2525, Manchester (061) 228 6311, Birmingham (021) 236 7000, London (01) 897 4000.

LOGANAIR: Kirkwall (0856) 3457, Inverness (0667) 62332, Glasgow (041) 889 3181, Edinburgh (031) 333 3338, Wick (0955) 2294.

2. *WHERE TO STAY*

Hotels in Orkney are quite inexpensive in comparison with mainland hotels. It is possible to get a twin room inclusive of a cooked breakfast for £12 per person upwards. Special rates can be negotiated for groups. Bed and breakfasts start at around £7 per night. There is a wide selection of self-catering apartments which, for groups, can work out at about £20 per person per week.

STROMNESS

Most of the dive-boats run out from Stromness which is the second largest town in Orkney and is its major seaport. Conveniently the ferry from Scrabster on the mainland calls in daily at about 2 p.m., leaving the next morning at 8.45 a.m. Many of the dive-boats berth in the picturesque harbour and will be only a stones throw from your accommodation. The harbour bustles and thrives with industry. 'Clamming' or scallop diving is carried on commercially from here. The town was originally built to serve the seafaring needs of its inhabitants and many of the original stone houses that fringe the harbour and bay still have their own small slips called 'nousts'. Stromness was formerly a whaling town and the Hudson Bay Company operated from here in the 18th century. The old town centre is very atmospheric with its meandering paved alleys. The town is well served by its own shops and hotels and has a swimming pool for those days when you fancy a dip in some warm water for a change.

(i) *THE FERRY INN*: As you come off the ferry, one of the first buildings you will see is the Ferry Inn. It is a delightful small hotel with 12 bedrooms. The owners have spent considerable time and thought in refurbishing this hotel to a high standard and it can cater for approximately 24 divers at any one time. The Ferry Inn is a warm, welcoming hotel and is very much a favourite with many divers who come back to Scapa Flow year after year. There are six rooms with private facilities, four rooms with a shower and wash-hand basin and two rooms with wash-hand basin only. All the rooms have colour TV and coffee-making facilities and there is an additional TV lounge.

The owners welcome divers and find it easier to cope with large parties of divers booking the whole hotel rather than having to mix divers with 'ordinary' tourists. There is a recently refurbished lounge bar which is popular with the locals and serves good bar meals and Guinness! It has an adjoining open-plan restaurant area serving extensive and reasonably priced meals to residents and non-residents alike. Local seafood dishes are its speciality.

There are no drying facilities for your gear but this will not present a problem as your gear can safely be left hanging up to dry on board your dive-boat.

Prices for single or double rooms are very reasonable with or without breakfast and a discount may be obtained for block booking. To book, telephone (0856) 850280.

(ii) *THE STROMNESS HOTEL*: This is the major hotel in Stromness and dominates the waterfront only yards from the ferry terminal. From here the main street meanders its way along the front and the town's many shops are all close by. The hotel is popular with locals and there is often a disco on a Friday night. Recently refurbished, it has 42 rooms all of which, bar five, have their own private facilities. The other five have wash-hand basins only. All the rooms have coffee-making facilities and most have a colour TV. In addition there is also a cosy TV lounge. The public bar and lounge bar serve hearty bar meals and there is a pool table and juke box. There is also a coffee shop and restaurant. There are no drying facilities for gear. The present owners welcome divers and will do special packages for block bookings. To book, telephone (0856) 850298.

(iii) *THE ROYAL HOTEL*: The Royal Hotel is to be found a short distance up Victoria Street, still in the old part of Stromness. It has a public bar with a pool table and juke box and a lounge bar serving bar meals at reasonable cost. There is also a separate dining-room. The hotel has 11 bedrooms all of which have recently been refurbished to a high standard and have their own private facilities. There is central heating throughout and colour TV in all bedrooms along with coffee-making facilities. There are two large rooms for drying and storing your gear. The present owners encourage divers and will give special rates for groups on enquiry.

Live music is arranged for most Friday and Saturday evenings and there is a late licence to 1 a.m. every night except Sunday. To book telephone (0856) 850342.

(iv) *THE OAKLEIGH HOTEL*: This hotel sits right on the waterfront in the old part of Stromness and has its own traditional slip at the back. It has long been a popular hotel for divers as the former owners ran one of the dive-boats. It has its own public bar and a comfortable new lounge bar has recently been opened. The accommodation comprises nine bedrooms which vary from single and double rooms to a larger dormitory-type room with bunk beds which can sleep seven to eight divers and is thus correspondingly cheaper per head. Only the large bedroom has a private shower but there are five separate bathrooms. Each week or two there is a video presentation on diving which draws a large crowd. To book, telephone (0856) 850447.

(v) *THE BRAES*: This is a family run hotel set, as its name implies, up the hill that rises from the water's edge at Stromness. It commands an unparalleled panoramic view out over Stromness, Scapa Flow and Hoy. The Braes has three double bedrooms, one twin room and two family rooms with bunk beds providing sleeping accommodation for four in each room. All the rooms have a private shower and washhand basin and two have an en suite toilet. Each room has its own tea/coffee-making facilities and colour TV. Extensive bar meals are served. There are several outhouses at the rear of the hotel which can be used for storing and drying diving gear. To book, telephone (0856) 850495.

(vi) *BED & BREAKFAST/GUEST HOUSES*: There are a multitude of small bed & breakfast and guest houses to cater for every taste and pocket, in and around Stromness, and many cater extensively for divers. If you want to stay in bed & breakfast accommodation then your dive-boat charterer will be able to make the necessary arrangements for you. Alternatively you should contact the Orkney Tourist Board at (0856) 2856 or 850716 and they will arrange suitable accommodation for you or will send you their detailed tourist information brochure which is packed with particulars and up-to-date costs.

BURRAY

Burray is one of the small eastern islands linked by the Churchill Barriers that now form an uninterrupted road all the way down the east of Scapa Flow to the southmost island, South Ronaldsay. The harbour area has its own slip and from here it is a good hour's motor in a hard boat to the main wreck sites. It is therefore equidistant with Stromness to the German wrecks. It is a more isolated area than Stromness but what it lacks in atmosphere it makes up for by having the Churchill Barriers literally right on its doorstep and so has easy access to the many wrecks up and down them.

(i) *THE SANDS MOTEL*: The Sands has a unique setting right beside the quay at Burray used by many of the dive-boats. From the accommodation it is less than ten metres to the quay to be picked up by your dive-boat in the mornings. Talk about convenience diving! The Sands has a fine outlook over a sheltered bay and it is a warm, welcoming place, popular with both locals and divers. Hearty bar meals are served to fill you up after a day's diving and there is a pool table, dart boards and a juke box. There is also a separate restaurant serving full meals. On most Friday evenings live music is arranged and there is a growing tradition of groups of divers doing their turn on the floor to the amusement of everyone. The dancing goes on well into the night and since Fridays are usually the last day's diving on a week trip there are no worries about getting up early the next day to dive. There is only the ferry at 8.45 a.m. to worry about!

The accommodation consists of four modern, six-person, self-catering flats each with three twin rooms with private sink, shower room with a wash-hand basin and toilet as well as a separate toilet with the usual facilities. A spacious lounge with colour TV serves as a meeting place and is open plan to the kitchen which is fully equipped with cooker, fridge, crockery and cutlery. All linen is provided and a laundry service can be arranged. The owners will buy in groceries and supplies for you prior to your arrival on request. To book, telephone (0856) 73 298

(ii) *SCAPA FLOW DIVING CENTRE*: Situated on the southmost part of Barrier No. 4 itself, the self-catering accommodation consists of two houses and two flats right on the shores of Scapa Flow and about 300 metres from several Barrier wrecks. The flats have one double bedroom and a bedsettee in the living-room/kitchen. The houses have three double bedrooms, bathroom, kitchen, living-room and a box room. About one mile away are another two houses with three and four bedrooms respectively. The accommodation looks out over the Flow and is fully fitted with shower and bath and kitchen with cooker, fridge, crockery and cutlery. The houses have open fires in the living-rooms and electric fires in the other rooms and the flats have electric fires throughout. Electricity is charged per unit used. Linen is provided and cots are available for small children. There is ample parking space outside and outside drying facilities. Cooked breakfasts and evening meals can be arranged with the proprietors on request as can baby-sitting, if required. Groceries and coal can be bought in prior to your arrival by contacting the owners. There is a garage, licensed grocer, bar and restaurant and a café, all within a mile of the accommodation. To book, telephone (0856) 73 225 or 253.

(iii) *THE COMMODORE MOTEL*: Situated not far from Burray in Holm the Commodore is a very attractive modern motel with a pleasant lounge bar and public bar serving well prepared and reasonably priced bar meals. The public bar has pool tables, dart boards and a unique 'weather centre'. A restaurant serves full meals.

The accommodation consists of six chalet units ideal for mixed or family groups. One of the units sleeps six or seven in single beds and is suitable for a diving party. To book, telephone (0856) 78 319.

KIRKWALL

Kirkwall is not so well placed for diving as Stromness and Burray although many divers do stay there. Scapa pier is only five minutes' drive away and so is an excellent pick-up point for the dive-boat. Kirkwall is certainly the most lively place in Orkney and thrives with shops, hotels, pubs and night life. If your dive-boat cannot pick you up from Scapa pier but is based in Stromness or Burray then this will entail a road journey of about 25 minutes first thing in the morning and back again last thing at night. Your dive-boat may be able to pick you up at Houghton Bay which is somewhat closer than Stromness. Kirkwall has a thriving tourist trade during the diving months and the hotels can be very busy. If you decide you want to stay in Kirkwall then ask your dive-boat skipper to arrange the accommodation to suit your pocket or alternatively contact the Orkney Tourist Office at (0856) 2856. There are simply too many to list here.

SCAPA FLOW DIVE CENTRES/DIVE-BOAT CHARTERS

1. *KEITH THOMSON, BOAT HIRE & DIVE-BOAT CHARTER.* Roadside, Widewall, South Ronaldsay.

Diving is from the 45-foot *Evening Star* which has a 16.5 cubic foot on-board compressor capable of speedily filling three bottles at once. The *Evening Star* is fully equipped with the latest technology of radar, navigator, echo-sounder and 65-channel VHF radio making the location of the deep German wrecks easy. On board there is a two-ring burner to heat up soup, tea and coffee on your return to the surface. The tea and coffee is free and very welcome on the colder days. There is a toilet and a heated drying room below decks which also doubles as a store for your gear overnight. No accommodation is available on board but the owners will arrange accommodation if requested to suit individual tastes from self-catering flats to hotels. Although based in South Ronaldsay, the owners are able to collect divers from any part of the Flow so accommodation does not have to be arranged in South Ronaldsay. Burray with its own pier and accommodation nearby is very convenient. The dive package includes the free use of 96-cubic-foot bottles, backpacks and weights although you will have to take your own weight belts. To book or obtain further details telephone (0856) 83 372.

2. *HIGH SEAS FLEET DIVING CENTRE.* 8 Dundas Street, Stromness.

The High Seas Fleet Diving Centre operates the 65-foot MFV *Sharon Rose* out of Stromness. The *Sharon Rose* is equipped with depth-sounder/fishfinder, 65-channel VHF radio, radar navigator, two-ton winch, toilet, colour TV and catering facilities. The changing room/drying room with shower is fully heated and offers ample space for 12 divers (the maximum permitted number of divers on any vessel) to kit up. She has an on-board 16-cubic-foot compressor to provide ample air. The dive package includes free use of 96-

cubic foot steel cylinders with backpacks and din fittings for UK divers and free use of all lead weights. The air fills are free too as is the welcome hot tea and coffee that awaits your return to the surface.

The Centre also caters for individuals and small parties. Accommodation can be arranged onshore or on the *Sharon Rose* herself. To book or obtain further details telephone 0856 850489.

3. *MARA DIVING CHARTERS.* Braehead Cottage, Stromness.

Mara Diving Charters is owned by George Litts, an experienced diver himself. Diving is from the 74-foot *Mara* which has an on-board 16-cubic-foot compressor. Again, 96-cubic-foot bottles and weights are available at no extra cost. In addition there are two canoes, two windsurfers and a clay pigeon trap available. Accommodation is provided on-board in 17 bunk beds in four cabins either self-catering, Bed and Breakfast or full board. Two cabins have six bunks, there is one four-berth cabin and a single cabin. There are two showers and two toilets, heated changing room, TV and video and a well equipped galley. To book or obtain further details telephone (0856) 850434.

4. *JOHN'S CHARTERS.* The Manse, Palace Road, Kirkwall.

Run by John Thornton, a well known local diver and one of the first to start charters, this long established dive charter was formerly known as 'Dive Orkney'. The 65-foot steel *Scapa Courier* based in Stromness provides the transport and other facilities necessary to ensure great diving. The *Scapa Courier* has a large aft cabin and toilet and forward cabin with cooker, crockery, sink, seating, changing room and gear drying area. The boat is equipped with VHF, radar, Decca navigator, sounders along with an on board 10-cubic-foot compressor and five-cubic-foot back-up compressor. The 16 steel 94-cubic-foot bottles are included in the price as are air fills and lead weights. Weight belts themselves are not included and divers should take their own.

Accommodation is not available on board but arrangements will be made to suit each party's requirements and pocket. To book or obtain further details telephone (0856) 4761.

5. *NORTH ISLES DIVING.* Spengar, Sandwick.

David Spence, who runs North Isles Diving, was one of the

first to set up diving in Scapa Flow and has been taking divers on to the wrecks of Scapa Flow for many years. The dive-boat is the 52-foot *Radiant Queen* based in Stromness. An on-board 7.8-cubic-foot compressor provides your air fills. Accommodation on-board is available in the six bunks on board although it is preferable for accommodation to be arranged onshore. Accommodation from self-catering flats to hotels will be arranged on request. There are 14 steel 94-cubic-foot bottles, back packs and weight belts available on board for use at a small extra charge. The *Radiant Queen* has on board catering facilities and piping hot tea and coffee is provided. There is a heated changing room and gear storage/drying area. In between dives, fishing or sight-seeing can be arranged.

David Spence owns four wrecks of his own in the Flow, namely the *F 2*, *UB-116*, *James Barrie* and HMS *Roedean*. (He bought the right to these wrecks many years ago.) To book or obtain further details telephone (0856) 84654.

6. *NORTHERN LIGHTS DIVING*. Eynhallow, Orquil Road, St Ola.

Northern Lights Diving no longer have their own dive-boat but can arrange diving holidays and accommodation. To book or obtain further details telephone (0856) 3974.

7. *ORKNEYINGA CHARTERS*. Walliwall Cottage, St Ola.

Orkneyinga Charters' ketch *Sula Sgeir* is a 56-foot ocean-going yacht designed specially for chartering and really provides a different way to dive, not just Scapa Flow but also to get out to many lesser-known wreck sites around Orkney, Fair Isle, North Rona and Sule Skerry.

With four double cabins, three single bunks and one double, there is accommodation for up to eight guests. Two cabins have en suite showers and toilet and a third shower/toilet is shared. The vessel is fully equipped with air compressor, bottles with backpacks and weight belts. Between dives there are facilities for wind surfing, clay-pigeon shooting, fishing or for those who just want to relax after a dive there is a TV, cassette player and library. To book or obtain further details telephone (0856) 5489.

8. *SCAPA FLOW DIVING CENTRE*. Burray.

The 47-foot *Shalder* is the main dive boat for the Scapa Flow Diving Centre which is located at Burray right on Barrier No. 4. An on board 15.5-cubic-foot compressor provides all the air you need with an additional onshore 18-cubic-foot compressor. Well equipped to cater for all a diver's needs, she has on board catering facilities and hot tea and coffee is provided. There is a large kitting-up room. Although the maximum number of divers on any one dive-boat is restricted to 12, the Centre does have other boats available for hire and can take parties of up to 40. There are bottles, backpacks and weights available for hire.

No accommodation is available on board the *Shalder* but is provided in self-catering houses and flats at Burray itself, only 300 metres from five Barrier wrecks which are ideal for night dives or when bad weather makes diving on the German Fleet impossible. Alternatively other accommodation can be arranged to suit individual tastes. To book or obtain further details telephone (0856) 73 225 or 253.

9. *DAVIE SCOTT.* 24 Nicholson Street, Kirkwall.

Diving is from the recently refitted 50-foot MV *Crombie* which can work out of any of the Scapa Flow ports. Fully equipped with VHF radio, radar, navigator and sounder, the *Crombie* also has an on board compressor. Twelve 98-cubic-foot bottles with backpacks and weights are included in the cost, but divers should bring their own weight belts. The *Crombie* boasts a spacious heated forward changing room which is also used for gear storage. There is a dry after cabin, toilet and shower. Tea and coffee are provided from the fully equipped galley. There is accommodation on board for eight people and accommodation onshore can be arranged on request. To book, or obtain further details, telephone (0856) 5047.

10. *P. STOUT.* Balay Cottage, Inganess Road, Kirkwall.

Diving is from the 65-foot dive-boat *John L.* All weights, bottles and air are provided. To book or obtain further information telephone (0856) 3157 or 4725.

11. *STROMNESS DIVING CENTRE.* Barkland, Cairston Road, Stromness.

Diving is from the 58-foot *Triton* which is based in Stromness. She is well equipped with radar, VHF radios, Navstar navigator and coloured meter with bottom lock. For those colder days there is a heated changing room and also a shower and toilet. There is a hold for storage and a cabin with six berths. In addition there is a large top cabin with cooker, table and seats. On board there is an 11-cubic-foot compressor and onshore there is a 15-cubic-foot compressor.

Included in the price are 87-cubic-foot cylinders and weight belts. Accommodation can be arranged onshore to suit everyone's pockets. To book or obtain further details telephone (0856) 850624.

12. *SUNRISE CHARTERS*. Holm Stores, St Mary's, Holm.

Diving is from the 70-foot MV *Sunrise* based in Stromness and specially converted to accommodate divers. Accommodation on board can be arranged in the six twin-berth cabins each with hot and cold water. There is a spacious heated lounge with TV and dining facilities for 12. The galley is well equipped with cooker, microwave oven and deep freeze. There are two hot showers, two toilets and a large drying room. Alternatively accommodation can be arranged onshore as required. There is an 11.5-cubic-foot on board compressor and 12 87-cubic-foot bottles; backpacks and weight belts are included at no extra cost. An inflatable is available for shallower dives and there is a clay pigeon launcher for divers wanting to bring their own guns and clays. To book or obtain further details telephone (0856) 78 393.

13. *TERRY TODDS*. Victoria Street, Stromness.

Diving is from the 50-foot *Girl Mina* based in Stromness. The *Girl Mina* is fully equipped with echo sounder, navigator and VHF radio and a 12-cubic-foot on board compressor. Twelve 72-cubic-foot cylinders are provided along with weights but divers should remember to take their own belts. There is a heated changing room and separate drying room, toilet and shower. A fully equipped galley provides meals and all the hot tea and coffee throughout the day. There is sleeping accommodation aboard for 12 divers and alternative onshore accommodation can be arranged. To book or obtain further details telephone (0856) 851034.

This is not an entirely complete list of the dive-boat charters working in Scapa Flow. Boats and businesses are bought and sold and new businesses are setting up periodically as the boom in diving at Scapa Flow continues to draw more and more divers each year. Further details of charters can be obtained by contacting the Orkney Tourist Board at 6 Broad Street, Kirkwall, telephone (0856) 2856 or at the Ferry Terminal Building, Stromness, telephone (0856) 850716.

Bibliography

Bowman, Gerald, *The Man Who Bought a Navy*, George G. Harrap & Co. Ltd, 1964.

Brown, Malcolm & Patricia Meehan, *Scapa Flow*, Allen Lane, The Penguin Press, 1968.

B.S.A.C. Wreck Register.

Burrows, C. W., *Scapa and a Camera*, Country Life, London, 1921.

Cousins, Geoffrey, *The Story of Scapa Flow*, Frederick Muller Ltd, 1965.

Cox, E. F., *Eight Years Salvage Work at Scapa Flow*, 1932.

Die Deutsche Flotte 1848–1945, Lohse-Eissing Verlag, Wilhelmshaven, 1962.

Dönitz, Karl, *Der Kreig Sur See*, Mittler & Sohn, 1966.

Dönitz, Karl, *Memoirs: Ten Years and Twenty Days*, Weidenfeld & Nicolson, London, 1958.

Esher, Reginald Viscount, *The Tragedy of Lord Kitchener*, John Murray, London 1921.

Ferguson, David S., *The Wrecks of Scapa Flow*, The Orkney Press, 1985.

Ferguson, David S., *Shipwrecks of Orkney, Shetland and Pentland Firth*, David & Charles plc., 1988.

Gardiner, Leslie, *The Royal Oak Courts Martial*, William Blackwood & Sons Ltd., London, 1965.

George, S. C., *Jutland to Junkyard*, Patrick Stephens, Cambridge 1973.

Hewison, William S., *This Great Harbour Scapa Flow*, 1985.

Howarth, David & the Editors of Time-Life Books, *The Dreadnoughts*, Time-Life Books, Amsterdam, 1979.

Korganoff, Alexandre, *The Phantom of Scapa Flow*, Ian Allan Ltd, 1969.

Marder, Arthur J., *From Dreadnought to Scapa Flow*, Oxford University Press 1970.

Morris, Keith & Peter Rowlands, *Exploring Shipwrecks*, Windward, 1987.

Macdonald, James, *Churchill's Prisoners. The Italians in Orkney 1942–1944*, The Orcadian Ltd, Kirkwall.

McKee, Alexander, *Black Saturday*, Souvenir Press, London 1959.

Naval Staff Monographs (Historical), Volume XVII. Public Record Office, Richmond, Surrey.

The Orcadian Newspaper, 1918–1940.

Public Record Office: Admiralty: War of 1939–1945.

ADM 199/158X/J5845 Loss of HMS *Royal Oak*—Board of Enquiry.

ADM 199/158X/K1651 Narrative of events in *Royal Oak*.

Conclusions & Recommendations of the Board.

BIBLIOGRAPHY

ADM 1/9840X/J5823 Report on Rescue Work & Assistance to Officers & Men.

Reuter, Ludwig Von, *Scapa Flow*, 1940.

Roskill, S. W., *The War at Sea*, Vol I. Collins, London, 1960.

Royle, Trevor, *The Kitchener Enigma*, Michael Joseph Ltd, 1985.

Ruge, Vice-Admiral F., *Scapa Flow 1919*, Ian Allan, London, 1969.

Smith, Peter L., *The Naval Wrecks of Scapa Flow*, The Orkney Press 1989.

Synder, Gerald S., *The Royal Oak Disaster*, William Kimber, 1976.

Taylor, I. D. M., *The Salvaging of the Ex-German High Seas Fleet at Scapa Flow* (1924–1939), 1963.

Taylor, J. C., *German Warships of World War I*, Ian Allan, London, 1971.

The Log of the U-47, 15 September-21 October 1939. (British Admiralty Translation.)

Vat, Dan van der, *The Grand Scuttle*, Hodder & Stoughton, 1982.

Weaver, H. J., *Nightmare at Scapa Flow*, Cressrelles Publishing, 1980.

INDEX

A.C. 6, 119

Alloa Shipbreaking Company, 50

Almeria, 119

Aorangie, 116

Archangel, Northern Russia, 134, 136

Argyle, 119

Armistice, 16, 18, 19, 28, 29, 30, 31, 74

B-98, 32

Baden, 22, 25, 33

Barrell of Butter, 82, 89

Bayern, 20, 26, 27, 50, 53, 96/97

Bendall, Sick Berth Attendant, 132

Blockships, 12, 60, 106–125

Blohm & Voss, 83, 98

Bottle Dive, 104

Braes Hotel, 148

Bremen, 77

Bremse, 19, 26, 46, 81

Brough of Birsay, 138

Brummer, 11, 26, 53, 54, 56, 57, 81–83, 97

Budrie, 113

Burra Sound, 60, 61, 64, 106, 108–113

Burray, 63, 65, 113, 122, 149

Busk, 116

Cape Ortegal, 119

Carron, 122, 123

Cava, 24, 25, 89, 93

Chiocchetti, Domenico, 114

Churchill Barriers, 60, 107, 113–120

Clio, 126

Clonsin, 26, 89

Collingdoc, 123, 124

Commodore Motel, 150

Cox & Danks, 34

Cox, Ernest, 34, 35, 36, 37, 39, 40, 42, 43, 44, 45, 46, 47, 48, 49, 50, 51, 95

Crombie, MV, 154

Daisy II, MV, 129, 131

Decompression, 61

Derfflinger, 15, 50, 68

Dive-boat Charterers, 62

Diving Practice, 63

Doyle, 60, 64, 106, 112

Dreadnought, HMS, 54

Dresden, 11, 15, 26, 53, 54, 56, 57, 81, 87–90

East Weddel Sound (No. 3 Barrier), 106, 119–122

Ehlers, Lt-Cdr, 21

Elton, 117, 118

Emden, 18, 19, 20, 21, 24, 25, 26, 33

Emerald Wings, 119

Empire Seaman, 120, 121

Ems, river estuary, 73

Equipment, 59

Evening Star, MV, 151

F 2, 64, 100/102

Fara, 23, 105

F/C Pontoon, 119

Ferry Inn, 147

Firth of Forth, 42, 43

Flanders, 73

Flotta, 56, 57, 102

Forth Railway Bridge, 44

Frankfurt, 19, 26, 33

Fremantle, Sir Sydney, 22, 25, 28, 31

Friedrich Der Grosse, 21, 24, 50

G 38, 36

G 91, 36

G 102, 24

G 104, 37

Gartshore, 120, 122

General Strike, 37

Germaniawerft Shipyard, 70, 100

Girl Mina, MV, 155

Glims Holm, 113, 120

Gobernador Bories, 60, 64, 106, 110-11

Gondolier, 126

Gourko, HMS, 141

Grace Paterson Ritchie, Kirkwall Lifeboat, 99

Grand Fleet, 15, 18, 19, 67, 69, 73, 136, 140

Grosser Kurfürst, 25, 50, 71

INDEX

Gutter Sound, 104

Hampshire, HMS, 64, 134–140
Harbours, Department of, 56, 57
Helgoland, 73, 74
High Seas Fleet Diving Centre, 151
Hindenburg, 15, 34, 37, 38, 39, 41,
  46, 47, 49, 95
Hipper, Admiral, 71
Houghton Bay, 65
Howaldtswerke Shipyard, 87
Hoxa Sound, 98, 99, 106, 138
Hoy, 23, 24, 63, 78, 138

Ilsenstein, 118
Imbat, HM Drifter, 105
Inchcolm, 44
Inverlane, 60, 64, 106, 107, 108/109
Iron Duke, HMS, 102
Italian Chapel, 114

J 1, 71
James Barrie, 99/100
Jellicoe, Admiral, 68, 77, 136, 138, 140
John L, MV, 154
John's Charters, 152
Juniata, 126
Jutland, Battle of, 16, 67, 71, 77,
  127, 136, 140

Kaiserliches Werft Shipyard, 67, 90
Karlsruhe, 11, 26, 53, 54, 81, 90–94
Kaiser, 45, 46
Kaiser Wilhelm II, 54
Kaiserin, 50
Keith Thomson, Boat Hire & Dive-
  boat Charters, 151
Kiel, 70, 74, 87, 100
Kirk Sound (No. 1 Barrier), 106,
  107, 114/116
Kirkwall, 128, 150
Kitchener, Lord, 134–140
Kitchener Memorial, 135
Köln, 11, 15, 26, 53, 54, 55, 56, 57,
  81, 83–87, 97
König, 11, 15, 50, 53, 66–71, 73, 74,
  77, 97
Kronprinz Wilhelm, 11, 15, 50, 53,
  67, 70–77, 97

Lamb Holm, 113
Lapland, 120, 122
Laurence, Commander Noel, 71, 73
Lisboa, 32

Longhope, 102
Lorne, 126
Louther Rock, 99
Lusitania, 71
Lützow, 68
Lycia, 118
Lyness, 24, 25, 42, 46, 63, 64, 78,
  95, 100, 104, 105

McLean, Captain, 25
Mara, MV, 152
Mara Diving Charters, 152
Markgraf, 11, 23, 53, 67, 68, 70, 71,
  73, 74, 77–81, 97
Martis, 120, 122
Marwick Head, 134, 138
Metal Industries, 50, 96, 119
Moltke, 15, 26, 33, 39, 41, 42, 43, 44
Motor Torpedo Boat (MTB), 105

Naja, 126
Nebbi Geo Creek, 139
Nichols, Captain R. F., 140
Nigg, 28, 29, 30
North Isles Diving, 152
Northern Lights Diving, 153
Numidian, 114
Nundy, Arthur, 50
Nundy (Marine Metals) Ltd, 50, 70
Nürnberg, 26, 33

Oak, HMS, 136
Oakleigh Hotel, 148
Orkney Harbour Area Bye-Laws
  1977, 56
Orkneyinga Charters, 153

Pan Hope, 99
Pegasus, HMS, 129, 132
Pentland Firth, 127, 136
Photography, 60
Plankton bloom, 57
Pontos, 123, 126
Prien, Gunther, 107
Prinzregent Luitpold, 49, 50
Prudentia, 102

Quoyness, 99

Radiant Queen, MV, 153
Ramillies, HMS, 27
Ramna, HM Drifter, 33, 34
Reginald, 120, 121, 122

Reuter, Rear-Admiral Ludwig von, 15, 18, 19, 20, 21, 24, 25, 26, 28, 29, 30, 31, 32, 33
Resolution, HMS, 28
Revenge, HMS, 26, 28, 29
Rheinfield, 119
Robertson, J. W., 33, 36
Roedean, HMS, 102
Ronda, 113
Rosewood, 119
Rosyth, 42, 43, 50
Rotherfield, 113
Royal Hotel, 148
Royal Oak, HMS, 12, 56, 64, 107, 114, 127–133
Rysa Little, 94
Rysa Lodge, Gutter Sound, 100

S 36, 96
S 52, 36
S 53, 36
S 54, 96
S 55, 36
S 65, 37
S 132, 25
S 137, 23
Sands Motel, 149
Scapa, 56, 57, 99, 127, 128
Scapa Courier, MV, 152
Scapa Flow Diving Centre, 150, 153
Scapa Flow Salvage & Shipping Co Ltd, 33
Schilling Roadstead Anchorage, 73
Schumann, Lt-Cdr Walther, 23, 77, 78
Schwieger, Kapitanleutnant Walther, 71
Scott, David, 154
Scrabster, 106, 143, 144, 145
Scrapyard, High Seas Fleet, 97
Seaforth Highlanders, 30
Seydlitz, 15, 26, 34, 44, 45
Shalder, MV, 153
Sharon Rose, MV, 151/152
Skagerrak, Battle of, 67
Skaill Bay, 139, 140
Skerry Sound (No. 2 Barrier), 106, 117–119
South Ronaldsay, 98, 108, 113, 122, 145
Stettin, 81
Stout, P., 154

Stromness, 33, 63, 65, 143, 144, 145, 146
Stromness Diving Centre, 154
Stromness Hotel, 147
Sunrise, MV, 155
Sunrise Charters, 155
Swanbister Bay, 104
Sula Sgeir, 153

Tabarka, 60, 64, 106, 111/112
Teeswood, 119
Terschelling, 73
Thames, 116
Thames Estuary, 73
The Times, 31
Third Battleship Squadron, 67, 71, 77
Tirpitz, Alfred von, 54, 73
Thüringen, 73, 74
Thurso, 143
Todds, Terry, 155
Tor Ness, 138
Treaty of Versailles, 18, 32
Triton, MV, 154

U-20, 71
U-47, 107
U-75, 140
U-135, 73
UB-116, 53, 98/99
Unity, HMS, 138
Urmstone Grange, 113

V 70, 35, 36
V 83, 11, 94-96
V 127, 23
Vanguard, HMS, 11, 56, 64, 140–142
Vegar, HMS, 22, 23
Vegesack, 108
Vesper, HMS, 22, 23
Victor, HMS, 138
Vickers Shipyard, Barrow, 141
Victorious, HMS, 22, 25
Von der Tann, 15, 48, 49, 50
Vulcan, A. G. (Shipyard), 81, 94

Water Sound (No. 4 Barrier), 106, 122–126
Weser, A. G., 77
Widewall Bay, 99
Wilhelmshaven, 32, 67, 90

YC 21, 102